Investment Timing
and the
Business Cycle

WILEY FRONTIERS IN FINANCE

SERIES EDITOR: EDWARD I. ALTMAN, NEW YORK UNIVERSITY

Investment Timing and the Business Cycle

JON GREGORY TAYLOR

John Wiley & Sons, Inc.

New York • Chichester • Weinheim • Brisbane • Singapore • Toronto

Library of Congress Cataloging-in-Publication Data:

Taylor, Jon Gregory.
    Investment timing and the business cycle / Jon Gregory Taylor.
       p.   cm. — (Wiley frontiers in finance)
    Includes index.
    ISBN 0-471-18879-4 (alk. paper)
    1. Investments. 2. Securities. 3. Business cycles. I. Title.
II. Series.
    HG4521.T35   1997
    332.6—dc21   97-8632

Printed in the United States of America

10 9 8 7 6 5 4 3 2 1

To My Father

Acknowledgments

Throughout my professional career, I have benefited from the association of many colleagues who have contributed to my knowledge and understanding of the economy and financial markets. Their insights are indirectly reflected throughout the text and are gratefully acknowledged. I would particularly like to cite Gary Hufbauer, who was my boss at the U.S. Treasury Department, for his very significant contribution to my early career development. I am also grateful to Gary Brinson and Jeffrey Diermeier at Brinson Partners for introducing me to investment management.

I have also benefited from access to the research product of numerous brokerage and investment houses including Goldman Sachs, J.P. Morgan, Merrill Lynch, Kidder Peabody and Barclays de Zoete Wedd to name a few. I have been particularly influenced and impressed with the quality of economic research from Goldman Sachs, J.P. Morgan and Merrill Lynch.

Several individuals were directly involved in the preparation of the text and should be acknowledged. Julian Reeves and Chris Mears both made extensive comments and suggestions on significant portions of the text. Julian also contributed to the conceptualization of some of the methodologies employed in the analysis and was my informal consultant on numerous issues. Silvana Lau provided the methodology for assessing seasonality in the major global equity markets. David Chai, Deborah Collins, Chris Johnson and Fiona Rossi-Mel all provided research assistance.

J.G.T.

Contents

CHAPTER 4   KEY U.S. ECONOMIC INDICATORS AND THEIR INTERPRETATION

List of Exhibits

Introduction

The business cycle—which articulates the evolution of the economy through time—provides the fundamental backdrop for investment returns. Financial markets are acutely sensitive to economic conditions and to changes in these conditions. Various classes of assets perform very differently under different economic conditions and to exploit the opportunities presented by these disparate conditions the investor must understand the dynamics of the economy and how changes in the economy impact different categories of investments.

This primer offers a framework for assessing and understanding the business cycle and its impact on different types of financial assets. The text provides global and regional "maps" of the business cycle; identifies the linkages between the real economy and financial markets; explores the transmission mechanisms; identifies the key variables that should be monitored and provides insights into how and when the business cycle impacts asset prices. This work is not intended to be the definitive tome on econometric techniques or equations for forecasting the economy or the financial markets; rather, it is an exploration of how changes in the economy affect financial assets.

The business cycle is dynamic. External events such as the oil price shocks of 1973 and 1979 can alter the course of the business cycle with dramatic consequences for financial markets. Historically, the cycle has been dominated by housing and autos. In the nineties, however, the cycle has been dominated by technology, with information technology paramount. This cycle has witnessed continually falling prices in key component areas in the technology sectors, such as microprocessors, despite ever increasing demand. At the same time, wages and salaries in these sectors have increased sharply. The traditional nexus of increasing demand and rising prices has been broken.

Clearly, the traditional cycle has evolved and needs to be recalibrated, but no one should be lulled into believing that the cycle is dead; it is just more complex, presenting investors with more risk and more opportunities should they assess the cycle correctly.

BUSINESS AND GROWTH CYCLES

Financial markets are inextricably linked to the real economy. All rational investment decisions contain explicit or implicit judgments about current and future economic conditions. Consequently, the departure point for any market timing decision is an assessment of the state of the economy, the position of the economy within the business cycle, and the predicted trajectory of the economy going forward.

It is the business cycle which captures and articulates the evolution of the economy through time, and thus holds the key to successful market timing. For the U.S. economy, the National Bureau of Economic Research (NBER) defines the business cycle and oversees much of the research into the economy's dynamics. Increasingly, attention has shifted from more formal business cycle analyses with the emphasis on recessions, to a focus on growth cycles—that is, deviations around trend or sustainable noninflationary growth—as more relevant to monitor. Both approaches are useful and meaningful in their own right. Additionally, minicycles at the sector level are becoming increasingly important because the economy is often subject to a series of rolling minicycles that tend to mute and/or moderate the overall cycle.

The growth cycle has gained significance because of policy makers' focus on concepts such as the non-accelerating inflation rate of unemployment (NAIRU) which specifies the "natural rate" of unemployment in the economy based on rigidities within the labor market rather than overall demand conditions within the economy. This concept, argued separately by Milton Friedman and Edmund Phelps[1] in the late sixties, contends that below a certain point (defined by the NAIRU), the growth–inflation trade-off is void because labor market rigidities

[1] Friedman, Milton, "The Role of Monetary Policy," American Economic Review, March 1968, 1–17. Phelps, Edmund, "Phillips Curves, Expectations of Inflation, and Optimal Unemployment Over Time," *Economics,* August, 1967, 254–81.

constrain further declines in unemployment. Thus, given the importance of the NAIRU, which can obviously change through time, macroeconomic policy and particularly monetary policy, focuses on deviations around trend or sustainable noninflationary growth. Thus, by monitoring the growth cycle, investors can glean insights into policy decisions that are likely to impact financial markets.

Growth cycle analysis focuses on the output gap which measures the difference between actual growth over time and potential growth. In a very real sense, the output gap provides a measure of capacity within the system and thus provides an excellent measure of the potential for real expansion or contraction. That is, excess demand and supply within the economy can be assessed and the implications for financial markets can be divined.

MONITORING ECONOMIC CYCLES

Economies are constrained by the availability of capital and labor. The production function specifies the potential output of the economy by modeling the projected growth in the factors of production, based on the existing stock of capital and labor. Deviations in potential growth—whether specified by the production function or simply by a regression trend of past growth—imply an output gap that can be either positive or negative and has clear implications for financial markets as the economy either moves further from equilibrium or returns to equilibrium. An understanding of where the economy is at any given point relative to its potential provides valuable insights into the likely impact that the future course of the economy will have on asset prices. For example, a significantly negative output gap implies falling prices, accommodative monetary policy, significant excess capacity and an ideal time to invest in equities. Conversely, a strongly positive output gap implies excess demand, constrained capacity, inflationary pressure, restrictive monetary policy and a negative time for equities.

Financial markets are acutely sensitive to economic data because of their usefulness in assessing the state of the economy. The significance of economic data and information depends on the timeliness of the data, the accuracy of the data versus subsequent revisions, the importance of the data for assessing the overall situation and, finally, the impact the release of new data has on financial markets. The more powerful the information (in terms of assessing the course of the economy), the more impact its release is likely to have on the markets and on asset prices. Releases such as the National Association of Purchasing Managers Survey (NAPM), capacity utilization and the employment report are all closely scrutinized by market participants because of their importance in confirming the state of the economy.

PHASES OF THE BUSINESS OR GROWTH CYCLE AND ASSET RETURNS

A business or growth cycle can usefully be divided into four major phases: (1) economic expansion from below trend growth to a "normal" rate of growth; (2) economic growth above a sustainable noninflationary level; (3) a cyclical peak in growth, followed by a decline in the rate of growth toward the trend rate and (4) growth falling below trend toward a cyclical trough. From an investor's perspective, each phase of the cycle has relevant implications for relative returns to different asset classes.

Financial assets are acutely sensitive to these phases of the cycle. Equities perform best when the economy is operating below potential and experience their strongest performance months before the economy emerges from recession. Bonds also perform best when the economy is operating below capacity and inflation is abating. Bonds perform worst when the economy moves from trend growth to growth above trend or above the sustainable noninflationary growth trajectory. Growth above trend implies inflation which, by definition, is the kiss of death for bonds. Cash outperforms equities only when the economy passes a cyclical peak and turns down. Cash outperforms bonds in a rising inflationary environment.

THE STOCK MARKET AND ECONOMIC CYCLES

The equity market is driven by earnings. The level and growth of earnings and profits are determined by the long-term secular growth trend of the economy and the progression of the economy through the business cycle. The outcome of a long-term "buy and hold" equity investment strategy would be dominated by trend growth. An investment strategy that entails market timing would be influenced by secular growth in the economy and by earnings variability, which is determined, at the aggregate level, by swings in the business cycle. The potential for enhancing investment returns in the equity market through market timing and business cycle analysis is significant, given the extreme swings in corporate profitability through the cycle.

The limited ability of corporations to significantly vary their capacity in the short run explains much of the variability in earnings and profits and holds the key to equity market timing. As excess capital and labor is utilized early in the cycle, corporate profitability increases substantially up to the point where capacity constraints emerge and exert higher costs on corporations. The move from a position of excess capacity to full capacity utilization greatly reduces costs per unit of output and creates a direct flow-through to earnings and profits.

The leveraging effect on corporate earnings caused by changes in the level of capacity utilization explains a significant portion of the stock market cycle. Near the trough of a recession or the lowest point of a growth cycle, corporations have slashed variable costs and the positive effects of rationalization are beginning to emerge and impact the bottom line. At this point, corporations are lean and mean but have high fixed costs. Once past the trough, capacity utilization increases as demand picks up. Fixed costs per unit of output are reduced and earnings increase. As demand accelerates and idle capacity continues to diminish, the leveraging effect on earnings and profits continues until capacity constraints begin to emerge and exert higher marginal costs on corporations.

THE BOND MARKET AND THE BUSINESS CYCLE

The Federal Reserve Board (the Fed) reigns supreme in the global bond market. That is, the U.S. central bank dominates global bond markets through its management of policy rates in the United States. The Fed acts in response to its reading of the current and future state of the economy and inflationary pressures within the system. A tertiary consideration, mandated by Congress, is the level of unemployment. The United States dominates global bond markets by virtue of the sheer size and diversity of its own bond market and the vast sums of capital raised by the federal government and by American corporations and households. All other bond markets benchmark off the U.S. bond market. The key to global interest rates is therefore embedded in the internal dynamics of the growth and business cycles in the United States and in the Fed's response to changes within the U.S. economy.

Even though global bond markets benchmark off the U.S. bond market, the spread or interest rate differential between the U.S. market and other markets depends critically on the position of each economy relative to other economies. There is a matrix of bond markets in which each bond market is related to every other bond market according to the stage of the respective business cycles. The stage of each countries business cycle relative to every other country is critical. Suppose the German economy is expanding at a rate above its long-term potential and inflationary pressures are beginning to emerge because of capacity constraints, while France, for whatever reason, is operating below potential and in a generally deflationary environment. In this environment, one would expect, *ceteris paribus,* the differential between French and German interest rates of comparable maturities to widen. That is, French interest rates will decline and German interest rates will increase.

Structural conditions play an important role in determining both the level and the direction of global interest rates. In general, countries with structural—as opposed to cyclical—current-account and government deficits incur a "risk premia" on their bonds relative to countries with balanced or surplus accounts. The overall external debt level also influences rate differentials. These structural considerations tend to evolve slowly and require major "sea changes" in governmental policy before they can impact relative interest rates. They therefore tend to be factored into the equation as a static given and are changed only infrequently, as a result of major initiatives. The Maastricht Treaty,[2] which

---

[2] The Maastricht Treaty, which constituted a major revision to the constitution of the European Union (EU), was negotiated in 1991 at Maastricht, the Netherlands, and entered into force in late 1993.

set out the convergence criteria required for monetary union and participation within the European Monetary System, is an example of a policy initiative that mandated major changes in macroeconomic policy and, as such, had an impact on structural risk premia within the global bond market.

A further complication is introduced by the foreign exchange market. Except for fully hedged investors, global bond investors make country allocation decisions based on expectations about the direction of both interest rates and exchange rates. Like interest rates, currency exchange rates are heavily influenced by business and growth cycles. The macroeconomic factors that tend to drive interest rate movements also loom large in currency markets.

To cite an example of the importance of the cyclical position of one economy relative to another, consider a case where one economy experiences robust growth and its trading partners experience moderate to stagnant growth. The growing economy will tend to experience import growth, but its exports will stagnate because of the lack of growth among its trading partners' economies. The resulting deterioration in the trade and current account will often be accompanied by a concomitant decline in the exporting country's exchange rate, even though its economy is strong. This was clearly the case with the U.S. dollar relative to the Japanese yen in the first half of the decade. The U.S. economy was registering strong growth while the Japanese economy was stagnating. For an investor to accurately gauge the likely impact of exchange rate changes on investment options, an appreciation of the position of the domestic economy relative to foreign economies is critical.

1 Financial Markets and the Business Cycle

Arguably, the most important factor in determining successful market timing is understanding the impact of the business cycle on various types of assets during different phases of the cycle. Powerful economic forces underpin asset class returns and unless these are understood and factored into investment decisions, performance will be suboptimal. A stylized depiction of the business or growth cycle and the relative performance of the major asset classes (equities, bonds and cash) is presented at Exhibit 1.1.

Exhibit 1.1 Business Cycle and Investment Returns.

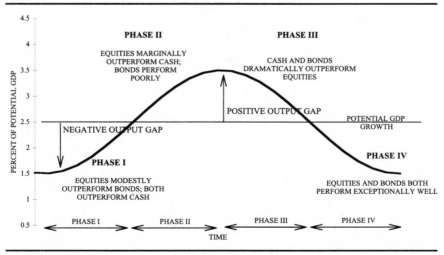

PHASES OF THE BUSINESS/GROWTH CYCLE AND ASSET RETURNS

The four phases of the business/growth cycle impact asset classes differently because of the dynamics of the economy during each phase. A brief overview of the impact of the growth cycle on different types of financial assets is presented in this chapter. Chapters 3 and 4 present an in-depth methodology and monitoring system for ascertaining where the economy is at any given point.

Exhibit 1.2   Phases of the U.S. Growth Cycle and Asset Returns.

	First Quarter 1970 to Second Quarter 1995 (Standard Deviation in Parentheses)			
	Phase I	Phase II	Phase III	Phase IV
	Negative & Decreasing (Narrowing) Output Gap	Positive & Increasing (Widening) Output Gap	Positive & Decreasing (Narrowing) Output Gap	Negative & Increasing (Widening) Output Gap
U.S. Balanced Portfolio*	10.8 (3.5)	6.0 (3.7)	3.8 (7.0)	19.9 (6.3)
S&P 500	11.4 (4.5)	8.1 (5.7)	1.0 (8.8)	22.5 (8.0)
U.S. Government Bonds	9.9 (3.2)	2.8 (3.0)	8.0 (6.5)	16.1 (6.6)
U.S. Small Cap Stocks	18.2 (8.9)	9.2 (8.7)	−7.4 (9.8)	29.6 (13.3)
Global Equities	11.2 (5.4)	13.0 (4.9)	−2.6 (10.2)	22.6 (8.9)
Commodities	6.3 (6.2)	23.6 (5.1)	19.9 (10.8)	−3.76 (7.3)
Cash	5.6 (0.6)	6.5 (0.3)	8.25 (0.4)	8.1 (0.7)

An increasing output gap is a gap that is moving further away from potential. A decreasing output gap is a gap that is moving in the direction of potential.

*Equities 60 percent and bonds 40 percent.

Data Source: Goldman Sachs & Co.

Phase I: Equities and Bonds Outperform Cash

During Phase I of the growth cycle, the economy is moving from the bottom of the cyclical trough toward a level of economic activity that is on a par with the sustainable noninflationary growth trajectory of the economy. Equities and bonds both perform relatively well during this phase, with equities modestly outperforming bonds. Both equities and bonds outperform cash. Balanced portfolios perform in line with equities and bonds. Commodities underperform equities and bonds but roughly match cash returns. Phase I is the second most attractive period for holding financial assets.

Phase I is often characterized by a resurgence of growth led by inventory accumulation and business investment. Housing construction, with attendant strength in consumer durables, is often an additional factor of strength. Given that rising demand can be met with existing capacity, corporate margins expand and translate into improvement in earnings growth at a rapid rate. Cyclical stocks tend to lead the advance with small cap stocks performing exceedingly well.

At this juncture, monetary policy often remains accommodative despite the surge in growth as significant excess capacity is present in the system and inflation tends to remain subdued. In fact, early in the expansion phase, inflation often continues to fall for some time despite the increase in activity. With inflation falling or stable and monetary policy very accommodative, bonds perform relatively well. Cash yields are normally low at this stage of the cycle given the accommodative stance of monetary policy.

Phase II: Equities Marginally Outperform Cash; Bonds Perform Poorly

In Phase II, the economy moves above its sustainable noninflationary growth path. Capacity constraints and labor shortages become evident in select industries and sectors. Inflation emerges as a problem.

Actual or foreshadowed early preemptive moves by the Federal Reserve Board (the Fed) to increase rates as a way of containing inflation result in a sell-off in the bond market and minimal returns accruing to bonds. In this phase, coupon income often just offsets capital losses because the inflation premium increases in tandem with real short-term rate increases orchestrated by the Fed. Returns to cash expand during this phase. Equities begin to flag as rising interest rates increase the discount factor for future dividends and the attractiveness of other investments, including cash, increases.

At this stage of the cycle, the demand/supply equation in the commodity market changes dramatically. Supply is constrained by existing capacity limits and demand accelerates along with economic acceleration. Commodities significantly outperform other asset classes. Precious metals are also bid up as a hedge against inflation.

Phase III: Cash and Bonds Dramatically Outperform Equities

In Phase III, growth moves from a cyclical peak to a below-trend level, prompting a narrowing of the output gap. This tends to be a dangerous phase of the cycle as policy responses aimed at moderating excessive growth often overcorrect and tip the economy into recession. The combination of tight monetary policy and inflation conspires to undermine equities. Small cap stocks lose ground relative to large cap stocks. Tight monetary policy and slowing economic growth provide a constructive backdrop for bonds, which basically return the coupon yield without any capital appreciation. Another result of tight monetary policy is higher cash returns. Capacity remains tight prompting commodities to register the strongest returns of any of the major asset classes. Market volatility is very high during Phase III.

Phase IV: Equities and Bonds Perform Exceptionally Well

Phase IV is characteristized by growth falling below potential with inflationary pressures abating and monetary policy becoming increasingly accommodative. Inventory correction is a major factor at this juncture which, once completed, provides the impetus for an inevitable upturn.

Equities actually register their highest returns during this phase of the cycle, in response to excess liquidity and anticipation of an upturn in the economy (with the attendant improvement in capacity utilization and margins). Bonds also perform best at this phase because the inflationary cycle is in a downward spiral accompanied by lax monetary policy. Cash rates decline from high levels and underperform both bonds and equities. Slack demand and excess capacity among commodity producers conspire to relegate commodity returns to negative territory. Commodities are the worst performing asset class in this phase of the cycle.

ECONOMIC FUNDAMENTALS AND ASSET PRICES

The key to understanding the impact of the business cycle on security returns is to understand the transmission mechanisms whereby changes in economic activity impact the factors that determine returns to various classes of securities.

Unquestionably, the optimal time for establishing a position in the stock market is at or near the trough in economic activity in any given cycle. At the end of March 1991—the trough of the November 1990 to March 1991 business cycle (as measured from peak to trough)—the S&P 500 was at 375.2. Over the next 68 months of expansion (to the end of November 1996), the S&P 500 moved to 757.0, a 101.8 percent capital gain which, when combined with dividend income, provided a total return of 135.8 percent for a compound annual total return of 16.4 percent. Over this period, consumer prices increased only 17.6 percent, for real returns of 118.2 percent or 14.8 percent per annum.

The inverse is generally true for bonds. The optimal time to hold bonds is when the economy is flagging and there are attendant expectations of falling inflation and looser monetary policy. Strong economic expansion, coupled with rising inflationary expectations, tends to cause bonds to sell off. This is particularly true when economic growth moves above the long-term sustainable rate, currently estimated at around 2.25 to 2.5 percent for the U.S. economy. For example, in 1993, when the U.S. economy moved from an annual growth rate of 2.6 percent for the six months ending in September to an annual rate of 6.3 percent in the December quarter, bonds sold off sharply. The yield on the U.S. 10-year bond went from 5.4 percent to a peak of 8.0 percent in November 1994.

A 10-year U.S. government bond would have incurred a loss of −3.2 percent over this period, with the coupon income from the bond offsetting, to some extent, the capital loss of 10.7 percent. The bond market sell-off of 1993–1994 was prompted by expectations that an overheated economy would cause mounting inflationary pressures. An additional concern was that the Fed would tighten monetary policy via an increase in short-term interest rates to "preempt" inflation. In fact, this is exactly what transpired.

The highest return from all assets except commodities is achieved when the economy is operating below potential and is on a negative trajectory. At this juncture, monetary policy is normally accommodative, and both interest rates and inflation are falling. An accommodative monetary policy provides the system with excess liquidity, which, although it ultimately stimulates real activity, initially results in asset price inflation. Accommodative monetary policy, in the form of excess liquidity and low policy rates, translates into capital gains in bonds as yields fall, in response to both lower policy yields and falling inflation caused by excess capacity in capital and labor markets.

At this point, corporate earnings are at depressed levels but are expected to recover on the back of a reflated economy with the initial pickup in demand met with existing excess capacity. The utilization of spare capacity permits an expansion of margins and improved corporate profitability. Equities, both domestic and international, perform exceptionally well. Small cap stocks show the highest returns given their positive cyclical bias. Bonds benefit from declining interest rates. Muted demand and excess capacity conspire to depress returns to commodities.

As Exhibit 1.3 (based on Goldman Sachs data) dramatically illustrates, asset returns are very dependent on the business or growth cycle of the economy. It is therefore imperative to understand the dynamics of the business cycle and to be able to ascertain where in the cycle the economy is at any given time, and what the likely trajectory will be as the economy goes forward. The business cycle not only shapes perceptions about the future performance of different classes of assets, it is also the major factor in determining valuation levels at any given time. The highest volatility is generally experienced at inflection points where the data on the economy are ambiguous and difficult to read.

Exhibit 1.3   Asset Returns and the U.S. Growth Cycle.

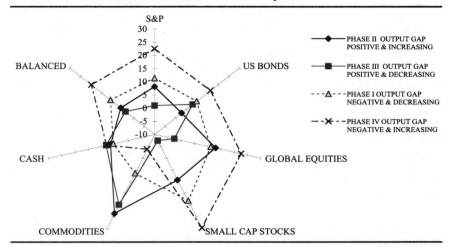

Asset Return Source: Goldman Sachs & Co.

RELATIVE PERFORMANCE OF EQUITIES VS. BONDS

Timing the allocation shift between asset classes can be fraught with difficulty. In hindsight, it is quite evident where the economy was in the cycle, but on a contemporaneous basis, it can be very difficult to determine the path of the economy. One of the most useful indicators of the overall status of the U.S. economy is the National Association of Purchasing Managers (NAPM) Index.[1]

The relationship between underlying economic performance—as proxied by the NAPM Index—and the performance of equities relative to bonds is depicted in Exhibit 1.4. Equities generally outperform bonds during phases when the economy is improving (a rising NAPM Index).

---

[1] The National Association of Purchasing Managers (NAPM) Survey is a comprehensive survey, based on a poll of over 300 purchasing managers, of trends in orders, production, employment, delivery times, inventories, and prices. The NAPM Index is a diffusion index. Readings above 50 are viewed as expansionary, and readings below 45 are often precursors to recession. The Index is published monthly. The lag between the Survey and the release of the results is about $2\frac{1}{2}$ weeks. The timeliness of the Index makes it extremely useful for gauging the economy.

Bonds outperform equities during periods when the economy is slowing
(a falling NAPM Index). The NAPM Index is particularly useful for
marking major turning points when the outperformance of equities re-
verts to bond outperformance, or vice versa.

The arrows on Exhibit 1.4 relate major turning points in relative performance and major turning points in the NAPM Index. Up arrows indicate an upturn in the NAPM Index and the beginning of equity
outperformance. Down arrows indicate a downturn in the NAPM Index
and the beginning of a period of bond market outperformance.

Peaks and troughs in the NAPM Index have generally coincided with
turning points in relative performance, but there have been significant
periods when other factors prevailed and the NAPM registered a false
signal. Nevertheless, turning points in the NAPM Index have given correct signals in 26 out of 30 major turns during the period from 1978 to
1996, or 87 percent of the time. Occasions when the NAPM Index gave
an incorrect signal or missed timing the crossover by a significant margin are noted with a double-sided solid arrow. The four major misses

Exhibit 1.4   NAPM Index and the Relative Performance of Equities vs. Bonds.*

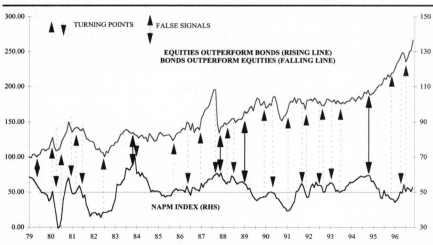

* Standard & Poor's 500 total return index versus the Merrill Lynch total return U.S. Government Bond Index.

RHS = Right Hand Scale

occurred: (1) in early 1979, when the NAPM Index began a one-year period of decline and equities continued to outperform bonds; (2) during the second half of 1983, when the NAPM Index advanced to just under 70 and bonds outperformed equities; (3) at the beginning of 1988, following the 1987 stock market crash, when the NAPM Index declined modestly during the first quarter but equities outperformed bonds and (4) in December 1994, when the NAPM Index began a significant decline that extended to the end of 1995, but the equity market outperformed bonds by a considerable margin. Several of these false signals can be explained by extenuating circumstances.

The outperformance of equities relative to bonds in the first quarter of 1988 (despite a declining NAPM Index) was due to the excessive nature of the October 1987 stock market crash, which made equities cheap and ripe for a period of outperformance once the trauma and volatility surrounding the crash had abated. It can be argued that 1995 was an extraordinary period during which corporate America engaged in ruthless cost control and profit preservation, which goes a long way toward explaining the break in the nexus between the NAPM Index and the relative performance of equities vs. bonds. An ancillary factor was the emergence of Internet stocks as high-growth stocks that drove the entire technology sector.

The NAPM Index does not always correctly signal a crossover in relative performance because the Index captures a single dimension of a multidimensional relationship.

Considerable discussion has recently surrounded the NAPM Index and its usefulness as a proxy for the economy as a whole given the increasing importance of the service sector of the economy. Despite this valid criticism, the NAPM Index remains one of the most timely and insightful indicators of the direction and performance of the economy.

HISTORICAL PERSPECTIVE

An assessment of the impact of the business cycle on asset returns necessarily needs to be put in the broader context of asset returns over time and across markets. Data prepared by Morgan Stanley shows the return on various assets in the United States since 1871, under different economic conditions (Exhibit 1.5).

During periods of price stability or falling inflation, equities have tended to outperform all other investments by a significant margin. During periods of rapid inflation, real assets such as houses and farmland

Exhibit 1.5   Asset Returns under Various Economic Conditions.

	CPI	Stocks	Bonds	U.S. T-Bills & Commercial Paper	Housing	Farmland	Gold	Silver
Deflation								
1871–1896	−1.5	5.5	6.4	5.4	N/AV	N/AV	*	−6.8
1892–1895	−3.3	−2.5	5.1	4.1	1.5%	N/AV	*	−8.0
1919–1922	−2.0	5.0	4.2	6.7	1.0	−12.1	*	−18.2
1929–1932	−6.4	−21.2	5.0	3.0	−3.9	−12.3	*	−19.8
Average	−3.3	−3.3	5.2	4.8	−0.4	−12.2		−13.2
Price Stability								
1896–1900	0.3	26.1	3.3	3.3	0.0	9.3	*	−1.0
1921–1929	−1.3	20.2	6.4	5.4	4.4	−2.8	*	−3.3
1934–1940	1.0	12.2	6.2	0.7	7.2	3.9	6.3%	1.0
1952–1955	0.3	24.5	3.5	1.5	4.5	6.5	*	2.1
Average	0.1	20.8	4.9	2.7	4.0	4.2		−0.3
Disinflation & Moderate Inflation								
1885–1892	0.0	4.5	4.4	5.1	N/AV	N/AV	*	−4.5
1899–1915	1.3	8.2	4.1	5.3	5.7	N/AV	*	−0.5
1942–1945	2.5	26.1	4.5	0.9	10.0	18.1	*	3.3
1951–1965	1.6	16.5	2.2	3.5	5.5	6.7	*	3.0
Average	1.8	14.3	5.9	4.3	6.3	9.8	−0.4	
1982–1995	3.6	16.4	14.3	6.6	3.9	4.5	−0.2	−3.4
Rapid Inflation								
1914–1919	13.3	11.6	2.1	4.7	17.5	14.7	*	15.5
1945–1947	6.8	12.3	2.6	1.0	12.2	18.5	*	8.6
1949–1951	5.8	24.8	0.9	2.3	10.2	21.7	*	20.5
1965–1971	4.0	6.4	6.1	6.8	10.3	12.7	31.6	23.7
1971–1981	8.3	5.8	3.8	8.8	10.3	14.6	28.0	21.5
Average	8.3	12.1	3.1	4.7	12.1	16.4	11.9	18.0

*Gold price fixed during these periods. NAV = not available.

Data Source: Morgan Stanley; Byron Wein, presentation material, Melbourne, Australia, 1996.

have outperformed equities, as have precious metals, which are the traditional hedge against inflation. Bonds and cash underperform other asset classes and also lag inflation during periods of rapid inflation.

Historically, bonds and cash have had the best relative performance during periods of deflation. Deflation was last experienced in the United States during the 1929–1932 recession.

Except during deflationary periods, equities have generally registered excellent investment returns.

COMPARATIVE GLOBAL RETURNS

The Group of Ten Deputies' compilation of real or inflation-adjusted returns for both debt and equity for the United States, the United Kingdom, France and Italy for the past 100 years[2] is shown in Exhibit 1.6.

The correlation of rates of return across countries and between instruments through time is remarkably high and undoubtedly reflects the

Exhibit 1.6   Historical Real Holding-Period Returns.

	Short-Term Debt				Long-Term-Debt				Equity			
	US	UK	FR	IT	US	UK	FR	IT	US	UK	FR	IT
1890s	5.8	2.4	2.5	3.6	4.5	4.2	3.6	6.1	7.2	6.7	2.8	2.9
1900s	2.6	2.3	2.8	2.2	0.5	−1.3	2.6	4.3	6.7	0.1	5.3	3.3
1910s	−1.1	−6.0	−9.0	−7.3	−4.0	−11.5	−12.2	−8.6	−1.2	−5.7	−7.9	−2.8
1920s	4.4	8.8	0.1	−1.9	8.8	7.0	4.2	−0.4	18.2	11.0	8.6	2.4
1930s	2.1	−0.2	−0.9	2.4	6.9	6.2	0.3	5.2	−1.1	6.5	2.7	9.6
1940s	−5.3	−1.5	−21.8	−30.0	−2.9	−0.4	−21.8	−28.0	2.1	2.6	−11.4	12.0
1950s	−0.6	−0.8	−1.8	−0.6	−3.3	−3.4	1.6	2.3	17.0	13.0	17.8	20.0
1960s	1.4	1.7	0.8	0.2	−0.7	−1.5	4.2	0.9	5.2	5.7	−0.3	0.8
1970s	−0.6	−4.8	−1.2	−3.8	−2.1	−4.5	−1.9	−4.8	−1.1	−1.3	0.8	12.0
1980s	3.0	4.7	4.1	0.6	6.7	7.4	8.1	2.4	10.7	14.0	12.4	14.0
1990s	1.1	6.2	7.3	3.5	8.2	6.3	12.1	8.2	6.5	6.6	13.0	−6.3
All	**1.1**	**1.0**	**−2.4**	**−3.6**	**1.6**	**0.6**	**−1.1**	**−2.1**	**6.2**	**5.2**	**3.0**	**1.8**

Data Source: Group of Ten Deputies, *Savings, Investment and Real Interest Rates,* October 1995, p. 20.

[2] Group of Ten Deputies, "Savings, Investment and Real Interest Rates," October 1995.

high level of integration of the economies of the four countries, and the simultaneous impact of major events such as the two World Wars.

SELECTED REFERENCES

Strongin, Steve, and Petsch, Melanie, "Asset Returns and the Economic Environment." *Commodity Research,* September 11, 1995. New York: Goldman Sachs & Co.

Group of Ten Deputies, "Savings, Investment and Real Interest Rates," October 1995.

2 Business and Growth Cycles

Economic growth in the United States has been highly uneven and prone to sharp swings, as Exhibit 2.1 illustrates. The amplitude of quarterly swings has moderated considerably in the post-World War II era, but significant swings persist and need to be monitored to achieve optimal market timing.

There are two useful ways of looking at changes in overall economic activity: classic business cycle analysis, with peaks, troughs and recessions; and the growth cycle, which monitors the economy from the perspective of deviations from trend growth. These two approaches both endeavor to provide insights into the dynamics of the economy and create a framework for understanding and monitoring economic cycles.

The macroeconomic theories that attempt to model and explain fluctuations in the business cycle are beyond the scope of this book. A brief synopsis of the main types of theories is presented in Appendix 2.1, at the end of this chapter.

BUSINESS CYCLES

Over the 137 years from 1854 to 1991, there were 31 full business cycles in the United States. Their average duration was 53 months. Since World War II, there have been nine cycles, of which seven have been peacetime cycles with an average duration of 53 months. The longest expansion since 1945 occurred during the Vietnam War and lasted 106 months, from February 1961 to December 1969. The shortest expansion lasted only 12 months, from July 1980 to July 1981. The longest peacetime

Exhibit 2.1   Business Cycles: U.S. GDP, Percentage Change on Previous Quarter 1875 to 1983.

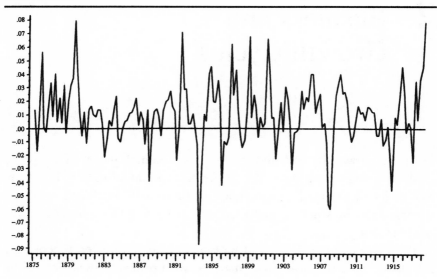

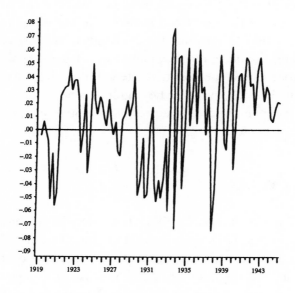

Exhibit 2.1 *(Continued)*

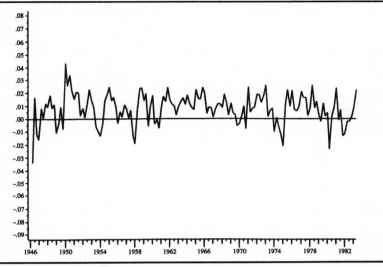

Data Source: Victor Zarnowitz, *Business Cycles: Theory, History Indicators, and Forecasting.* Chicago: National Bureau of Economic Research/University of Chicago Press, 1992.

expansion was the 92 months from November 1982 to July 1990. (See Exhibit 2.2.)

The National Bureau of Economic Research (NBER), a nonprofit organization of economic researchers, focuses on U.S. business cycles and is responsible for definitive pronouncements regarding segments and turning points of the business cycle.

Phases and turning points of the business cycle are generally characterized by the NBER as expansions, peaks, contractions and troughs. Downturns are further characterized as growth recessions, recessions and depressions.

Contrary to popular belief, the NBER does not define a recession as two consecutive quarters of decline in real GNP. The best short definition is provided by Geoffrey Moore, the dean of business cycle research: "A **recession** is a recurring period of absolute decline in total output, income, employment and trade, usually lasting six months to a year and marked by widespread contractions in many sectors of the economy."

Exhibit 2.2 U.S. Business Cycle Expansions and Contractions.

Business Cycle Reference Dates				Duration in Months			
				Contraction	Expansion	Cycle	
				Trough from Previous Peak	Trough to Peak	Trough from Previous Trough	Previous Trough Previous Peak
Trough		Peak					
December	1854	June	1857	—	30	—	—
December	1858	October	1860	18	22	48	40
June	1861	April	1865	8	46	30	54
December	1867	June	1869	32	18	78	50
December	1870	October	1873	18	34	36	52
March	1879	March	1882	65	36	99	101
May	1885	March	1887	38	22	74	60
April	1888	July	1890	13	27	35	40
May	1891	January	1893	10	20	37	30
June	1894	December	1895	17	18	37	35
June	1897	June	1899	18	24	36	42
December	1900	September	1902	18	21	42	39
August	1904	May	1907	23	33	44	56
June	1908	January	1910	13	19	46	32
January	1912	January	1913	24	12	43	36
December	1914	August	1918	23	44	35	67
March	1919	January	1920	7	10	51	17
July	1921	May	1923	18	22	28	40
July	1924	October	1926	14	27	36	41
November	1927	August	1929	13	21	40	34
March	1933	May	1937	43	50	64	93
June	1938	February	1945	13	80	63	93
October	1945	November	1948	8	37	88	45
October	1949	July	1953	11	45	48	56
May	1954	August	1957	10	39	55	49
April	1958	April	1960	8	24	47	32
February	1961	December	1969	10	106	34	116
November	1970	November	1973	11	36	117	47
March	1975	January	1980	16	58	52	74
July	1980	July	1981	6	12	64	18
November	1982	July	1990	16	92	28	108
March	1991			8	—	100	—

Average, all cycles:

1854–1991 (31 cycles)				18	35	53	53*
1854–1919 (16 cycles)				22	27	48	49**
1919–1945 (6 cycles)				18	35	53	53
1945–1991 (9 cycles)				11	50	61	61

Average, peacetime cycles:

1854–1991 (26 cycles)				19	29	48	48***
1854–1919 (14 cycles)				22	24	46	47****
1919–1945 (5 cycles)				20	26	46	45
1945–1991 (7 cycles)				11	43	53	53

*30 cycles; **15 cycles; ***25 cycles; ****13 cycles.

Data Source: National Bureau of Economic Research, Inc., published in the Survey of Current Business, October 1994, Table C-51.

Since World War II, recessions have decreased in frequency, duration and amplitude. In defining points in the business cycle, the focus of the NBER is on the overall level of economic activity.

A **growth recession** is a recurring period of slow growth in total output, income, employment and trade, usually lasting a year or more.

A **depression** is a recession that is major in both scale and duration. An example is the recession of 1929–1933.

Clear evidence, both anecdotal and statistical, is beginning to emerge to support the view that structural change in the U.S. economy over the past decade has helped to lengthen the business cycle and moderate the amplitude and duration of downturns when they do occur. American firms manage their inventories more aggressively with just-in-time and related systems that now allow better management of their inventory-to-sales ratio. At the end of 1995, the inventory-to-sales ratio was at the lowest level in 25 years. The new lean inventory management techniques moderate inventory buildup and, consequently, reduce inventory corrections, one of the major causes of business cycle downturns. In the current environment, corporate America is much more adept at managing tight production runs in response to contemporaneous demand, without allowing substantial unwanted inventory accumulation

In part, precise inventory management has been fostered by corporations' ability to gear up and gear down, adding and shedding labor more efficiently than they have been able to do in the past. In this new environment, corporations are not shy when it comes to firing redundant workers. Rationalization is very much in vogue.

The very tight timetables that are available for the delivery of business equipment—3 months vs. 6 months two decades ago—allow businesses to add capital to a flexible labor component with very little lead time. The bottom line is that there are fewer constraints to adding capacity when the economy turns upward. This reduces potential capacity constraints and potential inflationary pressure. In this new environment, capacity constraints are less rigid, thus reducing potential imbalances in the economy.

One of the most important changes in the structure of the economy has occurred in housing finance, and it has precipitated pronounced cyclical swings. The interest rate ceilings imposed on deposits prior to 1978 effectively capped mortgage lending whenever market rates exceed the ceiling. Conversely, when interest rates dropped below the ceiling, there was a flood of mortgage lending and housing activity accelerated sharply. This produced an environment of boom/bust in the housing sector, which accentuated swings in the economy. The final elimination of all ceilings, in 1986, combined with the emergence of mortgage securitization, has resulted in a significant reduction in the severity of the swings in residential construction.

The increasing openness of the U.S. economy, with imports and exports accounting for roughly 15 percent and 13 percent respectively, has also helped to moderate the economy's cyclical tendencies. That is, 13 percent of what the nation produces is to meet external demand, which, to a large extent, has a different cycle than domestic demand. High import penetration of the U.S. economy means that a downturn in domestic demand is shared by external suppliers. Additionally, strong external demand can provide meaningful stimulus to the U.S. economy at the margin.

GROWTH CYCLES

Given the declining frequency of full recessions in the post-World War II era, interest has shifted, to some extent, from business cycles to growth cycles. A growth cycle is often defined as pronounced deviations around the trend rate of economic growth. Growth cycles tend to be fairly symmetrical. Upturns last roughly 27 months and downturns last about 26 months (see Exhibit 2.3). Growth cycles tend to lead business cycles and, as such, they are useful precursors of major changes in the level of economic activity. On several occasions—1951–1952, 1962–1964, 1966–1967 and 1995, low-growth phases of the growth cycle represented midcycle pauses in the business cycle, and the cycle did not terminate. Midcycle pauses are normally characterized by a slowdown in economic activity in key sectors such as housing and manufacturing. Profit growth moderates but does not necessarily turn negative. Often, however, retardations in growth (below trend) result in the economy's slipping into recession. Growth cycles provide early warnings for recessions and for absolute declines in the level of economic activity.

Exhibit 2.3   U.S. Growth Cycles (1953–1995).

Upturns	Trough to Peak (Duration in Months)	Downturns	Peak to Trough (Duration in Months)
		Mar 1953 – Aug 1954	17
Aug 1954 – Feb 1957	30	Feb 1957 – Apr 1958	14
Apr 1958 – Feb 1960	22	Feb 1960 – Feb 1961	12
Feb 1961 – May 1962	15	May 1962 – Oct 1964	29
Oct 1964 – Jun 1966	20	Jun 1966 – Oct 1967	16
Oct 1967 – Mar 1969	17	Mar 1969 – Nov 1970	20
Nov 1970 – Mar 1973	28	Mar 1973 – Mar 1975	24
Mar 1975 – Dec 1978	45	Dec 1978 – Dec 1982	48
Dec 1982 – Jul 1984	19	Jul 1984 – Jan 1987	30
Jan 1987 – Feb 1989	25	Feb 1989 – Mar 1991	25
Mar 1991 – Dec 95 (P)	55		
AVERAGE	27.6	AVERAGE	53.5

P = Preliminary; no formal ruling by the NBER.

Data Source: National Bureau of Economic Research, Cambridge, Massachusetts.

As with business cycles, the NBER reviews consensus views on deviations from trend growth and sets out the chronology of growth cycles.

Growth cycles can be usefully divided into two phases: high growth and low growth, or above-average and below-average trend growth.

Numerous econometric techniques can be used to detrend growth, but the most useful application for assessing financial asset returns is a phase-average technique to allow for major structural shifts in the economy over time. Simple linear regression techniques can then be applied over appropriate time periods to determine the trend rate of growth of the economy.

A stylized depiction of economic growth cycles is presented in Exhibit 2.4.

The progression of the business cycle and/or growth cycle is of critical importance in determining returns to different classes of assets. For example, the stock market tends to be a leading indicator of economic upturns, and the bulk of the returns accrue to shares early in an economic upturn. Conversely, bonds tend to underperform during these

Exhibit 2.4   Stylized Economic Growth Cycles.

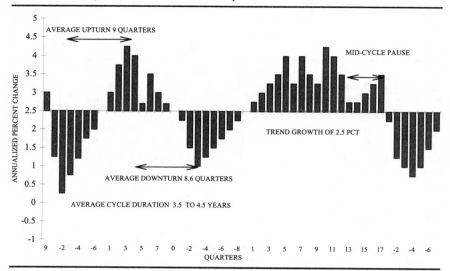

periods. In addition, different types of stocks perform differently during the various phases of the business cycle.

Significant deviations from trend growth can often induce macroeconomic policy responses that have very important implications for financial markets. For example, the commonly accepted sustainable level of growth for the U.S. economy is 2.25 to 2.5 percent. Growth above this level is assumed to stretch capacity and ultimately lead to inflation. Hence, growth significantly above trend for a measurable period of time can be assumed to prompt, for example, higher inflation and tighter monetary policy with attendant increases in interest rates. Rising short-term interest rates almost always lead to rising long-term interest rates and a sell-off in the bond market.

GLOBAL BUSINESS CYCLES

Increasingly, the performance of major economies is linked through trade and the flow of capital into financial assets. Synchronization of economic performance has increased, particularly among the major economies, but domestic factors can still derail an economy and cause it to move out of sync with the other major economies.

For global investors, monitoring the progression of various countries in terms of their relative position in the growth cycle suggests clear country-rotation strategies. That is, invest in countries that are at the trough of the growth cycle, and begin to reduce investments in countries just passing the peak of the growth cycle.

The Center for International Business Cycle Research (CIBCR) at Columbia University produces extensive research on global and international business cycles.

SELECTED REFERENCES

Niemira, Michael P., and Klein, Philip A. *Forecasting Financial and Economic Cycles,* New York: John Wiley & Sons, Inc., 1994.

Zarnowitz, Victor. *Business Cycles: Theory, History, Indicators, and Forecasting*. Chicago: National Bureau of Economic Research/University of Chicago Press, 1992.

Appendix 2.1 A Synopsis of Selected Business Cycle Theories.

| Type of Theory | Main Factors | | Are Cycles Linked to Growth? | Most Sensitive Processes | Special Features | Author and Dates |
	Originating	Responsive				
I. Some Largely Endogenous Theories						
Monetary disequilibrium	Unstable flow of money (bank credit)	Interest rate changes; cycles of inflation and deflation	No	Investment in traders' inventories	Cycles tend to be periodic under the gold standard	Hawtrey 1913–1937
Monetary overinvestment	Unstable supply of bank credit	Discrepancy between the natural and money interest rates	No, or weakly	Capital investment, lengthening and shortening of production processes	Real vertical maladjustments result from monetary disequilibria	Hayek 1931–1939
Cyclical real growth	Bursts of innovation (new products, markets, etc.) contested by imitators	Credit financing; excesses of speculation and misjudgment	Yes	Business capital investment booms and readjustments in contractions	Simultaneous interacting of long, intermediate, and short cycles	Schumpeter 1912–1939
II. Some Theories with Major Exogenous and Stochastic Elements						
Impulse and propagation in a real model	Undefined erratic shocks and discontinuous Schumpeterian innovations	Investment accelerator, lags in output of capital goods, money demand, and imperfectly elastic supply	Yes (through innovations)	Capital goods production, but the system as a whole is damped (dynamically stable)	Random shocks or innovations bunched in expansions needed to maintain oscillations	Frisch 1933

The original monetarist theory	Sequential shocks; high monetary growth rates followed by low rates, etc.	Relative prices and asset yields, then spending flows	Both consumption and investment react to monetary changes	No	Monetary policies destabilize the private sector	Friedman and Schwartz 1963a, 1963b
Market clearing with rational expectations and incomplete information	Random monetary shocks causing price-level variations	General price changes misperceived for relative price changes; intertemporal substitution of labor and leisure	Prompt and strong reactions to perceived changes in relative prices or real rates of return on the supply side	No	Flexible prices and wages clear markets continuously; money and price surprises cause fluctuations in output and investment	Lucas 1977
A disequilibrium theory of investment and financial instability (largely endogenous)	Unstable expected profits drive business investment, which generates fluctuations in realized profits	Money created by bank lending to business; short-term financing of long-term investment	Relative prices of capital assets set in financial markets under uncertainty about future returns, costs of capital, and cash flows	Yes	Long expansions produce overconfidence, unsound financing practices, a growing debt burden and illiquidity—all sources of contractions and crises	Minsky 1982

Data Source: Victor Zarnowitz *Business Cycles: Theory, History, Indicators, and Forecasting.* Chicago: National Bureau of Economic Research/ University of Chicago Press.

3 Monitoring the Business Cycle

Financial markets are leading indicators of economic activity and are, in fact, used as variables in many forecasting models. Financial market participants, however, are not as interested in forecasting the economy and business cycle per se as they are in understanding and predicting the impact of economic developments on financial assets. Successful exploitation of the business or growth cycle necessitates an understanding of the linkages in the macroeconomy and how changes in various sectors of the economy impact the overall evolution of the economic cycle.

SUSTAINABLE REAL GROWTH RATE AND THE OUTPUT GAP

The departure point for assessing the dynamics of the business or growth cycle is the long-run sustainable *real* growth rate of the economy. Economies are constrained by the capital and labor available for production. The availability and growth, over time, of these factors of production determine the long-term *potential* growth rate of the economy.

During recent decades, the sustainable noninflationary real growth rate for the United States was widely accepted to be around 2.5 percent per annum, which was set by an estimated annual labor force growth of 1.0 percent and labor productivity gains of 1.5 percent per annum. In fact, over the period from 1972 to 1995, trend real growth for the U.S. economy was 2.7 percent per annum. Under the new chain-linked methodology for measuring growth, introduced in early 1996, long-term real growth potential is probably closer to 2.0 to 2.25 percent.

Deviations in GDP growth from potential is either nonsustainable or suboptimal. Deviations from potential constitute the output gap for the economy. The existence of an output gap, by definition, indicates disequilibrium within the economy and implies inflationary or deflationary forces within the system.

The output gap is measured or estimated in several ways. After the fact, it is the observed difference between potential and realized GDP. Econometric techniques are used to estimate trend GDP growth and thus provide a basis for estimating deviation from trend. Exhibit 3.1 presents estimates of potential GDP from 1987 to 1995, using two regression techniques: the split time-trend methodology and the smoothing technique embodied in the Hodrick-Prescott filter. The split time-trend technique endeavors to measure trend growth for each discrete growth cycle. This technique allows trend growth to vary from cycle to cycle, but not during a cycle. The smoothing technique of the Hodrick-Prescott filter fits a trend through GDP over time but allows the coefficients to vary over time. Technically, this involves simultaneously minimizing a

Exhibit 3.1   OECD Estimates of U.S. Growth Potential and Output Gaps.

		Estimates of US GDP Growth Potential			Output Gaps under Different Methodologies		
	Actual	Split Time Trend Method	Hodrick-Prescott Method	Production Function Method	Split Time Trend Method	Hodrick-Prescott Method	Production Function Method
1987	3.1	2.6	2.9	2.5	1.0	0.7	0.2
1988	3.9	2.6	2.7	2.4	2.3	1.9	1.7
1989	2.5	2.4	2.5	2.0	2.5	1.9	2.2
1990	1.2	2.3	2.3	2.1	1.4	0.9	1.4
1991	−0.6	2.2	2.2	2.2	−1.4	−1.9	−1.4
1992	2.3	2.2	2.2	2.2	−1.3	−1.8	−1.3
1993	3.1	2.3	2.3	2.3	−0.5	−1.1	−0.4
1994	3.5	2.4	2.4	2.5	1.1	1.1	1.0
1995	2.1	2.4	2.4	2.5	−0.3	−0.3	−0.4

Data Source: Organization for Economic Cooperation and Development, "Potential Output, Output Gaps and Structural Budget Balances," by Claude Giorno, Pete Richardson, Deborah Roseveare, and Paul van den Noord. OECD Economic Studies No. 24, 1995/I. (Updated with final GDP numbers for 1994 and 1995.)

Exhibit 3.2 U.S Output Gap and Inflation.

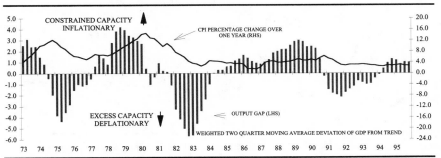

RHS—Right Hand Scale; LHS—Left Hand Scale

Data Sources: Gross Domestic Product—Bureau of Economic Analysis; CPI—Bureau of
Labor Statistics.

weighted average of the gap between output and trend output and the
rate of change of trend output at that point in time.[1]

The output gap can also be measured by estimating a production function for the economy and then measuring deviations from potential. Production functions generally take the form of an explicit model of
potential economic output, which is derived by measuring trend growth
in the factors of production and the existing labor and capital stock
within the economy. Potential real GDP, determined by changes in the
factors of production, has declined almost continuously, from above 4.0
percent in the sixties to the current level of 2.0 to 2.25 percent. The decline in potential real growth has several sources: a decline in labor
force growth in part due to a stabilization of participation rates; a decline in labor productivity growth, which fell from above 2.0 percent in
the sixties to the current level of around 1.0 percent.[2]

---

[1] Organization for Economic Cooperation and Development, "Potential Output, Output Gaps
and Structural Budget Balances," by Claude Giorno, Pete Richardson, Deborah Roseveare, and
Paul van den Noord. OECD Economic Studies No. 24, 1995/I. (Updated with final GDP numbers for 1994 and 1995.)

[2] Quarterly productivity can fluctuate substantially from quarter to quarter as economic
conditions change. For example, in the first quarter of 1997, productivity grew at an annual
rate of 2.8 percent while productivity fell 3.7 percent during the recessionary third quarter
of 1990.

Exhibit 3.3 Capacity Utilization and the Unemployment Rate.

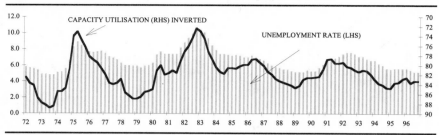

Data Sources: Capacity utilization—Federal Reserve Board; Unemployment Rate—Bureau of Labor Statistics.

A key concept in the estimation of potential output is the nonaccelerating wage rate of unemployment (NAWRU),[3] or the NAIRU or natural rate of unemployment (see p. 11), which arises from structural rigidities within the economy. In the United States, this level is widely estimated at around 5.5 to 6.0 percent. This is the unemployment rate that corresponds with an output gap of zero. Unemployment levels above or below this level imply falling or rising inflation respectively. That is, GDP growth below potential will result in falling inflation and GDP growth above potential will result in a buildup of inflationary pressures within the economy.

The capacity utilization level provides early indications about the level and sustainability of economic activity. The index covers an increasingly smaller share of overall activity within the economy, but because the manufacturing sector often sets the tone for the entire economy, it is important to monitor. In general, utilization rates above 85 percent have heralded upward pressure on prices while capacity levels in the high seventies have signaled softness in the economy and growth below potential.

It is important to know the magnitude of the output gap and whether the gap is increasing or decreasing as this has implications for monetary policy, interest rates and the future direction of the economy. The Federal Reserve Act gives the Fed the dual mandate of pursuing "stable

---

[3] The concept of the NAWRU was first explicitly introduced by J. Tobin in his seminal article "Inflation and Unemployment," in the *American Economic Review* in March 1972.

prices" and "maximum employment."[4] The output gap therefore provides the Fed with an important guidepost in the management of monetary policy.

The relationship between unemployment and inflation is captured by the Phillips Curve, which provides a formal framework for assessing the impact of the output gap on inflation or, more succinctly, the inflation/unemployment trade-off.[5] Excess demand for labor, as evidenced by a fall in the unemployment rate below the NAWRU, triggers an increase in price-level expectations, which, in turn, triggers higher wage demands and subsequently, a wage–price spiral. External shocks, such as the oil price increases of 1973 and 1979, can also produce inflationary spirals, even if the unemployment rate is below the NAWRU. In this instance, inflationary expectations were triggered by the oil price shock and validated later by rising wage demands. In 1979, the Federal Reserve's decision to apply the brakes with tight monetary policy pushed the economy into recession and broke the nexus between price expectations and price validation. The Fed's action stopped the inflation cycle but caused the unemployment rate to move above 10 percent by the end of the recession in 1983.

GROWTH CYCLE PHASES

The growth cycle can usefully be divided into four phases:

I. Expansion to potential.

II. Growth expansion above potential.

III. Contracting growth from nonsustainable levels.

IV. Contracting growth below potential.

Characterizing phases of the growth cycle and the dynamics of the economy at any given point is difficult because each cycle is unique.

---

[4] "Federal Reserve Act" 12 USC Section 226, December 23, 1913.
[5] A. W. Phillips, "The Relation between Unemployment and the Rate of Change of Money Wage Rates in the United Kingdom, 1861–1957," *Economica*, November 1958.

Nevertheless, useful generalizations and observations can provide guideposts for investors to monitor.

Phase I. Expansion to Potential

The beginning of phase I is identified by a trough in economic activity (Exhibit 3.4). The trough and subsequent upturn are normally heralded by the end of an inventory correction; that is, excess inventories have been worked off, and production has returned to near normal levels. A resumption of normal production results in an increase in hours worked, incremental employment creation and commensurate increases in disposable income and consumption.

Depending on the severity of the downturn, monetary policy is often very accommodative at this stage of the cycle and characterized by a steep yield curve with short-term rates substantially below long-term rates. Real short-term rates will probably be low and the spread between current inflation and the Fed funds rate will be less than 150 basis points. Inflation is quite subdued at this point in the cycle because the economy is operating below its potential, and considerable excess capacity is available in both the labor and capital markets. Lax monetary policy and the availability of cheap credit provide the impetus for an upturn in the housing market and for corporate expansion.

Exhibit 3.4   GDP Growth Cycle.

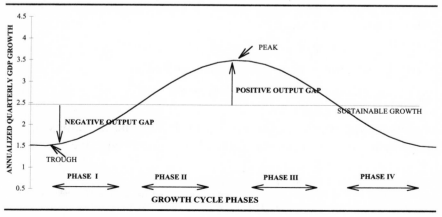

Phase I is characterized by the absorption of existing capacity in the system, but it is not associated with inflationary pressures because excess capacity exists in both the labor and capital markets at this juncture.

In this phase of the cycle, corporate margins tend to expand sharply because higher utilization of fixed capacity results in lower marginal costs. Strong corporate profitability and sharply increasing earnings per share translate into strong stock market performance.

Phase II. Growth Expansion above Potential

When growth accelerates above a sustainable level, the output gap turns negative, capacity constraints begin to emerge, and inflationary pressures begin to build within the system. Growth above potential generates inflationary concerns, which, if borne out by statistical evidence, causes weakness in the bond market as the market begins to anticipate a policy response in the form of higher interest rates from the Federal Reserve Open Market Committee (FOMC).

Early in this phase, a tug-of-war develops between earnings growth and expectations of higher inflation and higher interest rates.

The emergence of capacity constraints does, however, induce capacity augmentation. Investment in capital equipment accelerates as businesses endeavor to keep up with surging demand. During this phase of the growth cycle, capital goods producers tend to perform well.

At the peak of the cycle, interest and inflation fears clearly win out over earnings growth with the stock market weak to negative.

Phase III. Contracting Growth from Nonsustainable Levels

Even after the growth or business cycle has peaked, inflationary pressures persist. Firms continue to face capacity constraints that prompt upward pressure on the costs of production.

In this phase, monetary policy is generally restrictive. A flat to inverted yield curve signifies repeated increases in the Fed funds rate during the period. Growth persists above potential. In addition, long-term bond rates increase in response to higher inflationary expectations which are, in part, validated by the Fed raising the Fed funds rate.

The environment of tight monetary and credit policy will induce a pronounced downturn in the interest-sensitive segments of the economy such as housing and capital expenditures. These two sectors will lead the economy down.

Phase IV. Contracting Growth below Potential

Often, growth cycles in the United States have been determined by inventory cycles. Downturns are precipitated by inventory imbalances with excess inventories prompting manufacturing slowdowns. The slowdowns are normally accompanied by declines or sluggishness in business capital investment as excess capacity increases and the need for and profitability of investment activity diminish. The resulting impact on employment and consumer and business confidence precipitates a generalized slowdown.

A major precursor to a full-blown recession is an inverted yield curve, which occurs when short-term rates exceed long-term rates.

After the inventory imbalance has been worked off, however, the conditions for a resumption of normal growth are often in place.

Mid-Cycle Corrections

Mid-cycle pauses or corrections occur when a slowdown (but not a recession) in the economy of several quarters is followed by the resumption of strong, above-trend growth. The slowdown is normally characterized by anemic, but generally not negative, growth below trend. The pause often allows the economy to return to more normal levels, with output growth returning to a more sustainable medium-term trajectory. The key, from an investment perspective, is to divine whether the pause is just a pause, or whether it is a precursor to recession. The implications for investment decisions are radically different in the two scenarios.

A mid-cycle pause can be healthy both from a macroeconomic perspective and from the perspective of financial markets. A limited-duration slowdown from above-trend growth to below-trend growth provides a "breather" for stretched industrial production and capacity utilization. The moderation in production eases inflationary pressures in the system and delays the onset of the contraction phase of the monetary policy cycle, which generally ends or slows the phase of strong asset price appreciation.

Cyclical corrections are tricky from an investment perspective. They are difficult to divine with certainty and they represent high-risk investment decision trees. If the economy slips into recession rather than resuming a positive growth trajectory, then bonds outperform all other assets. However, if growth resumes, bonds are at risk given the already high levels of labor and capital utilization and the prospects of significant inflationary pressures building as further demands are placed on already stretched capacity. In this environment, commodities sharply outperform other assets given stretched capacity, inflationary pressures and the long lead times necessary to augment commodity supplies.

The case for equities is somewhat more ambiguous. The initial onset of a growth pause from above-trend growth is generally positive for equities because inflationary pressures ease with attendant expectations of or actual declines in short- and long-term interest rates. During the pause, declining interest rate expectations tend to dominate anticipation of a slowdown in earnings growth momentum. The resumption of growth following the pause improves the outlook for corporate earnings, but it raises the prospect of the onset of the contractionary phase of the monetary policy cycle. In general, equities perform relatively well, but they can become very sensitive to the direction of short-term interest rates.

SELECTED REFERENCES

Branson, William H. *Macroeconomic Theory and Policy,* 3rd ed. New York: Harper & Row, 1989.

Organization for Economic Cooperation and Development, "Potential Output, Output Gaps and Structural Budget Balances," Claude Giorno, Pete

Richardson, Deborah Roseveare, and Paul van den Noord. OECD Economic Studies No. 24, 1995/I.

Phillips, A. W. "The Relation Between Unemployment and the Rate of Change of Money Wage Rates in the United Kingdom, 1861–1957," *Economica,* Nov. 1958.

Tobin, J. "Inflation and Unemployment," *American Economic Review,* March 1972.

4 Key U.S. Economic Indicators and Their Interpretation

Economic fundamentals form the backdrop for asset markets and, indeed, ultimately determine financial asset returns. Financial market participants are increasingly called on to monitor economic indicators and interpret the data to determine the likely impact that new information will have on financial markets.

The focus is on the implications for growth and inflation. Growth determines profits and real returns while inflation features prominently in setting the discount that is embedded, explicitly or implicitly, in every investment decision.

The traditional business cycle indicators—leading, coincident and lagging—which historically were produced by the Bureau of Economic Analysis but are now produced by the Conference Board, are extremely useful in monitoring the economy and the business cycle. While these indicators are useful, the individual indicators and statistics that comprise these aggregate indicators are more timely and, in many ways, more helpful in monitoring the economy on a timely basis. The danger, of course, in looking at individual indicators is that they can be misleading when taken on a stand-alone basis over a one- to two-month period.

The major economic indicators for the United States are set out in this chapter, along with suggested ways of interpreting them in terms of divining the relevant phase of the business/growth cycle and the importance of the indicators to financial markets. Comments about their usefulness and reliability are also provided. For each indicator, the source, frequency, release day and time are presented in accompanying exhibits.

BUSINESS CYCLE INDICATORS

In 1996, the Conference Board, a business-sponsored research group, took over the task of producing and distributing the business cycle indicators that the Bureau of Economic Analysis of the U.S. Department of Commerce had, for decades, published on a monthly basis in the *Survey of Current Business.* These indicators included the composite leading, lagging and coincident indicators as well as the associated diffusion indices.

Over the years, business cycle indicators have been extensively reviewed and tested by Commerce Department economists, NBER-affiliated economists, academic economists and financial market affiliated economists. The Conference Board has committed to reviewing and updating the indices so that they remain relevant and timely.[1]

For the indicators to be useful singularly and in the aggregate, their relationship to the business cycle, in terms of both timing and interpreting the dynamics of the cycle, needs to be clearly understood. Indicators can most usefully be grouped into categories that collectively shed light on specific aspects of the cycle. "Business cycles . . . involve a great number of diverse economic processes and show up as distinct fluctuations in comprehensive series on production, employment, income and trade—aspects of aggregate economic activity."[2] Monitoring changes in these series should clearly provide insights into market timing and investment decisions.

The composite index of **leading indicators** is comprised of 10 equally weighted indicators that lead the economy:

---

[1] The components and calculation procedures for preparing the indexes were revised in December 1996 by the Conference Board. See "Business Cycle Indicators," Vol. 2, No. 6, June 1996, The Conference Board, New York, N.Y.

[2] Victor Zarnowitz, *Business Cycles: Theory, History, Indicators, and Forecasting.* Chicago: National Bureau of Economic Research/University of Chicago Press, 1992.

1. Average weekly hours of production workers in manufacturing.
2. Initial unemployment claims.
3. Manufacturers' new orders for consumer goods.
4. Vendor performance.
5. Plant and equipment orders.
6. Building permits.
7. S&P 500 Index of stock prices.
8. M2 money supply.
9. Interest rate spread, 10-year Treasury bonds less the federal funds rate.
10. Index of consumer expectations (University of Michigan).

Each of these leading indicators are described below.

The composite index of **coincident indicators** is comprised of only four indicators:

1. Employees on nonagricultural payrolls.
2. Personal income.
3. Index of industrial production.
4. Manufacturing and trade sales.

The composite index of **lagging indicators** has seven items:

1. Average unemployment duration.
2. Manufacturing inventories/sales ratio.
3. Changes in per-unit labor costs.
4. Prime rate changes.
5. Commercial and industrial loans outstanding.
6. Ratio of consumer installment credit outstanding to personal income.
7. Changes in the consumer price index for services.

Exhibit 4.1 Business Cycle Indicators.

Indicator	Source	Frequency	Date & Time
Leading, lagging and coincident economic indicators and related diffusion indices	The Conference Board	Monthly	Four weeks after month end. 10:00 A.M. EDT

Each of these composite indicators has a **diffusion index,** which measures the percentage of rising indicators relative to the total number of indicators.

For financial market participants, the focus is naturally on the leading indicators, but other indicators shed light on exactly where the economy is at any point in the cycle (Exhibit 4.1).

Conference Board graphs on the business cycle indicators are reproduced in Appendix 4.1 at the end of this chapter.

OUTPUT, PRODUCTION, ORDERS, INVENTORIES, SALES AND BUSINESS CONDITIONS

Gross Domestic Product (GDP), the broadest measure of the performance of the economy, is the total output of goods and services produced in the United States (Exhibit 4.2). The major components of GDP are: personal consumption; business investment in plant and equipment; inventories; residential investment; government purchases and net exports (exports minus imports). The data comprising the quarterly GDP report are generally widely known prior to its release. Advanced market estimates are generally fairly accurate; modest deviations produce only muted market reactions. Market attention is usually focused on the composition of growth and inventory swings.

The **Industrial Production (IP)** Index, produced by the Federal Reserve Board, measures manufacturing, mining and utility production, which accounts for roughly 26 percent of the output of the economy. The IP index is constructed from 264 individual series that use the 1987

Exhibit 4.2   Gross Domestic Product (1996).

	Billions of Dollars	Percent of Total
Private Consumption	5,151.4	68.0
Private Fixed Investment	1,117.0	14.7
Business Fixed Investment	791.1	10.4
Structures	214.3	2.8
Producers' Durable Equipment	576.8	7.6
Residential	310.5	4.1
Changes in Business Inventories	15.4	0.2
Net Exports of Goods and Services	−98.7	−1.3
Exports	855.2	11.3
Goods	614.9	8.1
Services	240.3	3.2
Imports	953.9	12.6
Goods	802.2	10.6
Services	151.7	2.0
Government Consumption and Gross Investment	1,406.4	18.6
Gross Domestic Product	7,576.1	100.0

Data Source: Survey of Current Business, June 1997.

Standard Industrial Classification (SIC) codes. The indices are season-ally adjusted. Manufacturing comprises roughly 86 percent of the index.

When interpreting the index, one needs to be particularly mindful that severe weather, natural disasters, strikes and holiday cycles can in-fluence the index and distort readings for short periods of time. Despite this caveat, market participants focus on monthly changes in the index and changes in the trend. The index is important in assessing swings in the business cycle, given the cyclical nature of the segments of the econ-omy that are represented in the index. Combined, the industrial sector and construction account for most of the variation in national output over the course of the business cycle.

Capacity utilization information is compiled for the manufacturing, mining and utilities industries by the Federal Reserve in tandem with the industrial production numbers. The utilization rate, expressed as a percent of capacity, is equal to an output index divided by a capacity (sustainable potential output) index. The index, which is seasonally adjusted, attempts to measure the sustainable practical capacity or the greatest level of output that a plant can maintain within a realistic work schedule taking account of normal downtime.

Capacity utilization rates above 85 percent are widely viewed as inflationary.

It is difficult to generalize about capacity utilization levels that characterize cyclical downturns, but sharply falling capacity utilization rates are associated with recessionary and/or declining growth periods within the economy. Recessionary troughs have generally seen capacity utilization rates below 78 percent and, on several occasions, utilization rates have reached the low 70s. Most recent recessionary troughs are marked by the trough in capacity utilization (Exhibit 4.3).

Four major surveys focusing on manufacturing activity and business conditions are conducted each month. The most important of these is the **National Association of Purchasing Managers (NAPM) Survey,** which has exceptional coverage and timeliness. The Chicago Purchasing Managers Survey, although limited in scope, is widely followed because it precedes the NAPM Survey by one day. The Philadelphia and Atlanta Federal Reserve Banks conduct surveys regarding business conditions in their regions.

The NAPM Survey canvasses 300-plus purchasing managers on trends in orders, production, employment, delivery times, inventories and prices. Each month, respondents are asked to characterize each

Exhibit 4.3   Capacity Utilization Rate.

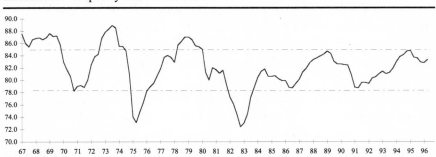

Data Source: Federal Reserve Board.

activity as being higher, lower or unchanged, compared to the previous month.

Indices for each of the components in the NAPM Survey are calculated, and a composite index, The Purchasing Managers Index (PMI), is constructed using the following weights: new orders, 30 percent; production, 25 percent; employment, 20 percent; delivery times, 15 percent and inventories, 10 percent. The indices are seasonally adjusted using the Department of Commerce adjustment factors.

In Exhibit 4.4, an overall PMI reading above 50 percent typically implies an expanding manufacturing sector, and a reading below 50 percent implies a contraction. Readings of 43.9 percent and below are normally associated with a decline in economic activity and recessions. The breakeven points for expansion and contraction vary among components. For employment, it is 47; for production, 50; for new orders, 51 and for inventories, 42 percent.

The NAPM Survey is one of the first reports to be generated each month and it is widely monitored as an early indicator of economic performance and direction. The report is particularly useful for its early information on production, employment, slack or tightness in the manufacturing sector and inventory levels.

The NAPM Survey also provides timely information on price trends in the manufacturing sector. The **suppliers' deliveries information** is a good indicator of delivery delays associated with bottlenecks and

Exhibit 4.4 National Association of Purchasing Managers Survey (NAPM)— Purchasing Managers Index (PMI).

Data Source: National Association of Purchasing Managers.

capacity constraints in the manufacturing sector, which reveal pricing power in the sector and inflationary pressures building in the system.

The **Chicago Purchasing Managers' Survey** is similar to the NAPM Survey, but respondents are confined to the greater metropolitan Chicago area. The overall index and the component indices are diffusion indices. Readings above 50 percent imply an expansion in manufacturing activity while a reading below 50 percent implies a contraction in manufacturing activity.

Like the NAPM Survey, the Chicago Purchasing Managers' Survey covers production, new orders, order backlogs, inventories, employment, supplier deliveries and prices. The Chicago Index often moves in the same direction as the NAPM Index, but it can occasionally take a divergent path. Essentially, it is a subset of the NAPM Index.

The **Philadelphia Federal Reserve Bank** and the **Atlanta Federal Reserve Bank** survey manufacturing firms in their respective jurisdictions (Pennsylvania, New Jersey and Delaware for the Philadelphia Fed and Alabama, Florida, Georgia and portions of Louisiana, Mississippi and Tennessee for the Atlanta Fed) on general **business conditions** and some specific activities. The responses are converted to diffusion indices centered on zero. Readings above zero reflect an improving situation and readings below zero indicate a deteriorating situation.

Activities surveyed include: new orders, shipments, unfilled orders, delivery time, inventories, prices paid, prices received, number of employees and length of the average employee workweek.

The Philadelphia Survey is by far the more important of the two given the relative concentration of manufacturing activity in that region versus the Atlanta region. Financial market participants focus almost exclusively on the Philadelphia Survey, although both surveys can indicate wide swings in overall business confidence. Over the period from October 1990 to September 1996, for example, the overall index of business conditions registered a high of 38.6 and a low of −48.1 (near the trough of the 1990–1991 recession).

The **"Beige Book" of Current Economic Conditions** is released eight times each year, just prior to the Federal Open Market Committee (FOMC) meetings, as part of the briefing material for the meetings. The Beige Book summarizes the economic and financial conditions reported by the 12 Federal Reserve district banks.

Its subjective, anecdotal presentation is useful only as a backdrop for the hard numbers emanating from other reports and surveys. Because the report is issued by the Federal Reserve Board, however, it is widely read by financial market participants.

The release of the statistics in the **Durable Goods Orders (advanced report)** is monitored and analyzed by the financial markets despite the difficulty in interpreting the numbers, the wide variations from month to month and the substantial subsequent revisions. The numbers are particularly difficult to analyze because of the lumpiness of the defense and aircraft components.

The Durable Goods Orders report covers manufactured products with a life expectancy over three years, plus estimates of shipments and unfilled orders. Durable goods account for roughly 15 percent of total economic output. The report can often provide critical insight into pressure building within the system or an impending slowdown in manufacturing activity. Consequently, it is an important barometer of manufacturing activity. The level of unfilled orders is particularly important in assessing the likely direction of industrial production.

The **Manufacturers' Shipments, Inventories and Orders** report is, in some respects, an expanded version of the information on durable goods released earlier. The report includes new orders, unfilled orders, shipments and inventories for durable and nondurable goods. Durable goods account for roughly 50 percent of the orders.

The inventory/shipments ratio, which can be gleaned from this report, is useful as an indicator of inventory imbalances building in the system. When they become extreme, inventory imbalances can precipitate sharp slowdowns or accelerations as companies attempt to redress the imbalances. Historically, pronounced inventory accumulation has preceded most recessions.

Manufacturing and Trade Inventories and Sales is a key report that indicates the level of retail, wholesale and manufacturing inventory and sales levels. The data are often substantially revised, however, and should be analyzed in terms of major shifts in accumulation or reduction rates. Automotive inventories are particularly volatile and need to be assessed against particular developments in the automotive sector. This report contains the all important inventories/sales ratio, which is a major indicator of imblances within the economy.

Exhibit 4.5 Output, Production, Orders, Inventories, Sales and Business Conditions.

Indicator	Source	Frequency	Date & Time
Gross Domestic Product (GDP)	Department of Commerce, Bureau of Economic Analysis	Quarterly	Eight weeks following quarter end. Revised twice, one and two months after the preliminary report. 8:30 A.M. EDT
Industrial Production (IP)	Federal Reserve Board	Monthly	Two weeks after month end. 9:15 A.M. EDT
Capacity Utilization	Federal Reserve Board	Monthly	Two weeks after month end. 9:15 A.M. EDT
National Association of Purchasing Managers' Survey (NAPM)	National Association of Purchasing Management	Monthly	First business day of following month. 10:00 A.M. EDT
Chicago Purchasing Managers' Survey	Purchasing Management Association of Chicago	Monthly	Last business day of the month. 10:00 A.M. EDT
Philadelphia Federal Reserve Bank Business Outlook Survey	Federal Reserve Bank of Philadelphia	Monthly	Third business day of each month. 10:00 A.M. EDT
Atlanta Federal Reserve Bank Business Outlook Survey	Federal Reserve Bank of Atlanta	Monthly	Various
"Beige Book" of Current Economic Conditions	Federal Reserve Board	Eight times per year, coincident with FOMC meetings	Second Wednesday before FOMC meetings. 12:00 P.M. EDT
Durable Goods Orders (Advanced Report)	Department of Commerce, Bureau of the Census	Monthly	Four weeks after month end. 8:30 A.M. EDT
Manufacturers' Shipments, Inventories, and Orders	Department of Commerce, Bureau of the Census	Monthly	Five weeks after month end. 10:00 A.M. EDT
Manufacturing and Trade Inventories and Sales	Department of Commerce, Bureau of the Census	Monthly	Six weeks after month end. 8:30 A.M. EDT

Stock levels are measured on a book value basis. Manufacturing sales are close to 45 percent of the total with retail and wholesale each 28 percent.

LABOR FORCE, EMPLOYMENT AND UNEMPLOYMENT

Three major gauges of labor market conditions are available: **Initial Jobless Claims Report, Employment Report** and **Help Wanted Advertising Index** (see Exhibit 4.6). The most timely of these is the weekly Jobless Claims Report, which contains data on newly unemployed individuals filing for benefits and on the number of people receiving unemployment benefits. The weekly report indicates initial claims with a 5-day lag and benefit recipients with a 12-day lag.

Both the initial claims and the ongoing benefits figures are useful in discerning changes in trends on a timely basis. The level of claims and the direction of change are important in assessing the likely impact on the all-important nonfarm payroll number. Because of the volatility of the numbers even with seasonal adjustment of the data, smoothing techniques such as moving averages are necessary when determining trends. (See Exhibit 4.7.)

Exhibit 4.6 Labor Force, Employment and Unemployment.

Indicator	Source	Frequency	Date & Time
Initial Jobless Claims	Labor Department, Employment and Training Administration	Weekly	Thursdays, 8:30 A.M. EDT
Employment Report	Labor Department, Bureau of Labor Statistics	Monthly	First Friday of following month. 8:30 A.M. EDT
Help Wanted Advertising Index	Conference Board	Monthly	Released just prior to employment report but with 5-week lag.

Exhibit 4.7   Payroll Growth and Initial Jobless Claims.

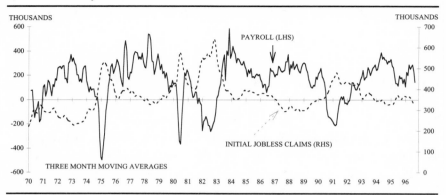

Data Source: Bureau of Labor Statistics.

Over the 10-year period from July 1986 to August 1996, initial job-less claims averaged 365 thousand per week. For the period from July 1991 to August 1996, they averaged 383 thousand per week.

The **Employment Report,** produced monthly by the Bureau of Labor Statistics, contains some of the most widely monitored and ana-lyzed numbers available on the U.S. economy. The survey, one of the most extensive surveys conducted in the United States, is the source of the **nonfarm payroll and unemployment** figures. Roughly 50 thou-sand households and just under 400 thousand companies with a total of 48 million employees—roughly one-third of all payroll employees—are surveyed. Data generated from this report are used in estimating industrial production, wages and salaries, personal income and capac-ity utilization.

Civilian **unemployment** statistics are used as a gauge of the tightness of the labor market and have serious implications for economic policy makers and the Federal Reserve. (For the U.S. economy, the non-accelerating wage rate of unemployment (NAWRU) is widely esti-mated to be between 5.5 and 6.0 percent.)

Changes in the **nonfarm payroll** numbers are used as an overall gauge of the pace of economic activity. Nonfarm payrolls increased an average of 175 thousand for the 10-year period from July 1986 to August 1996, and they have averaged 197 thousand for the more recent 5-year period. The nonfarm payroll numbers influence the calculation of personal income and consumption. Changes in **manufacturing payroll** numbers can be used to assess industrial production.

The index of **aggregate weekly hours worked** is an early indicator of expansion or contraction in GDP and can be used as a gauge of changes in real GDP. (This index includes overtime work.)

The **average hourly earnings** figures provide a measure of wage inflation and changes in personal income.

The **Help Wanted Advertising Index,** produced by the Conference Board, is also monitored, but the data in the report lag the Employment Report data by over a month, thus diminishing the value of the Index. The report has, however, been a leading indicator of peaks in total nonfarm payroll employment and serves as a proxy for changes in labor demand. The survey covers 51 major newspapers in 51 separate markets.

CONSUMER SPENDING, PERSONAL INCOME AND CONSUMER ATTITUDES

Consumer expenditures constitute 65 percent of the U.S. economy and are closely monitored because even small changes can have a significant impact. Financial markets tend to focus on the consumer sentiment surveys and leading retail sales indicators such as the weekly Johnson Redbook report. Financial markets are particularly sensitive to changes in retail sales and consumer expenditures because of what the changes imply for interest rates and Fed policy.

The two major consumer surveys are the **Consumer Confidence Survey,** conducted monthly by the Conference Board and the **University of Michigan's Consumer Sentiment Survey** (Exhibit 4.8). Both surveys focus on current conditions and expectations. The results of the Consumer Confidence Survey from 1969 through 1996 are shown in Exhibit 4.9.

Exhibit 4.8   Consumer Spending, Personal Income and Consumer Attitudes.

Indicator	Source	Frequency	Date & Time
Consumer Confidence Survey	Conference Board	Monthly	Last Tuesday of each month. 10:00 A.M. EDT
Consumer Sentiment Survey	University of Michigan Survey Research Center	Bi-monthly	Preliminary, Friday following the second weekend of the month. Final, Friday following the last weekend of the month. 10:00 A.M. EDT
Consumer Credit Report	Federal Reserve Board	Monthly	Five weeks after month end. Afternoon
Johnson Redbook Report	Johnson Redbook Service	Weekly	Tuesday. 2:55 P.M. EDT
Retail Sales	Commerce Department, Bureau of the Census	Monthly	Two weeks after month end. 8:30 A.M. EDT
Personal Income and Consumption Expenditures	Commerce Department, Bureau of Economic Analysis	Monthly	Four to five weeks after month end. 8:30 A.M. EDT

Exhibit 4.9   Consumer Confidence Survey.

Data Source: Conference Board.

Another closely monitored indicator of consumer activity is the **Consumer Credit Report,** generated monthly by the Federal Reserve Board. This report is useful in assessing consumer balance sheets and their capacity for funding consumer expenditures via installment credit. Extreme levels—either high or low—are of interest to the markets as an indication of consumer latitude in funding expenditures.

Because of its timeliness, the **Johnson Redbook Report,** which is published weekly, is widely viewed as an indicator of retail sales, even though it covers only department store sales, which constitute a small portion of total retail sales. The report, which has only a 3-day lag, estimates monthly sales based on cumulative weekly observations. The methodology can produce distortions early in the month, when the monthly estimate is based on a one or two week period. The report has a reputation for picking up shifts in the trend early.

The Department of Commerce publishes monthly reports on **Retail Sales** and **Personal Income and Consumption Expenditures.** Retail sales, including auto sales, account for somewhat less than half of all consumer expenditures and a little less than one-third of GDP. Personal consumption expenditures are an extremely important factor in overall GDP and personal income is the major determinant of personal consumption expenditures which account for 65 percent of GDP.

The Personal Income and Consumption Expenditures report includes information on the personal savings rate, stated as a percent of disposable income.

PRICES, WAGES, LABOR COSTS AND PRODUCTIVITY

The **Implicit GDP Price Deflator** measures the difference in current- and constant-dollar GDP. This method is linked to the old fixed-weight GDP measures. The **Chain-Weighted GDP Price Deflator** is linked to chain-weighted GDP. The indicator, by its nature, picks up changes in the composition of output as well as changes in prices over time.

The **Producer Price Index (PPI)** is compiled from a very broad survey of prices received by domestic producers during the month. The report includes three sets of indices: stage of processing; commodity

Exhibit 4.10   Prices, Wages, Labor Costs and Productivity.

Indicator	Source	Frequency	Date & Time
Implicit GDP Price Deflator	Commerce Department, Bureau of Economic Analysis	Quarterly	Eight weeks after quarter end. 8:30 A.M. EDT
Chain-weighted GDP Price Indexes	Commerce Department, Bureau of Economic Analysis	Quarterly	Eight weeks after quarter end. 8:30 A.M. EDT
Producer Price Index (PPI)	Labor Department, Bureau of Labor Statistics	Monthly	One to two weeks after month end. 8:30 A.M. EDT
Consumer Price Index (CPI)	Labor Department, Bureau of Labor Statistics	Monthly	Two weeks after month end. (Released after PPI) 8:30 A.M. EDT
Commodity Research Bureau (CRB) Indexes	Commodity Research Bureau	Daily	
Employment Cost Index (ECI)	Labor Department, Bureau of Labor Statistics	Quarterly	Four weeks after quarter end. 8:30 A.M. EDT
Non-Farm Business Productivity and Costs (Unit Labor Costs)	Labor Department, Bureau of Labor Statistics	Quarterly	Six weeks after quarter end. 10:00 A.M. EDT

group and industry. Market attention centers on the stage of processing, which is divided into crude, intermediate and finished.

Core intermediate goods prices are fairly good indicators of future finished goods prices, which in turn feed into consumer prices. The PPI, which tends to be a leading indicator of overall prices, receives considerable attention, even though it presents only part of the inflation picture.

The **Consumer Price Index (CPI)** measures retail prices for a fixed basket of goods and services. Major components of the index are food, housing, transportation, medical costs, clothing, entertainment and items in a "Miscellaneous" category. Economists and analysts often measured "core" inflation by excluding volatile food and energy components.

The **Commodity Research Bureau (CRB) Index,** produced daily by the Commodity Research Bureau, is the most widely followed commodity index. The CRB is an equal weighted index of 17 commodities: 9 agricultural commodities and 8 raw industrial material commodities. The breakdown of the index is as follows: Energy (crude oil, heating oil and natural gas) 18 percent; grains and oil seeds (corn, soybeans and wheat) 18 percent; industrials (copper and cotton) 11 percent; livestock (live cattle and live hogs) 11 percent; precious metals (gold, platinum and silver) 18 percent; soft commodities (cocoa, coffee, orange juice and sugar) 24 percent.

Other commodity indices are available and, depending on the particular issue, can be more useful than the CRB.

The **Employment Cost Index (ECI),** which measures changes in wages, salaries and benefits, is a very accurate measure of overall changes in workers' compensation. Because the index is broken down into wages and benefits, both costs can be accurately assessed. (See Exhibit 4.11.)

As discussed earlier, **average hourly earnings** also provide insights into wage inflation.

On a quarterly basis, the Department of Labor produces measures of **Non-Farm Business Productivity and Unit Labor Costs.** Economists pay considerable attention to the trend in unit labor costs, because labor

Exhibit 4.11   Employment Cost Index and the CPI.

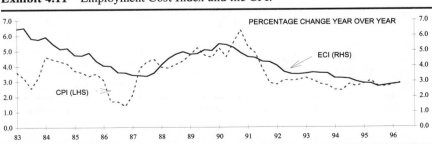

Data Source: Bureau of Labor Statistics.

Exhibit 4.12   Unit Labor Costs and the CPI

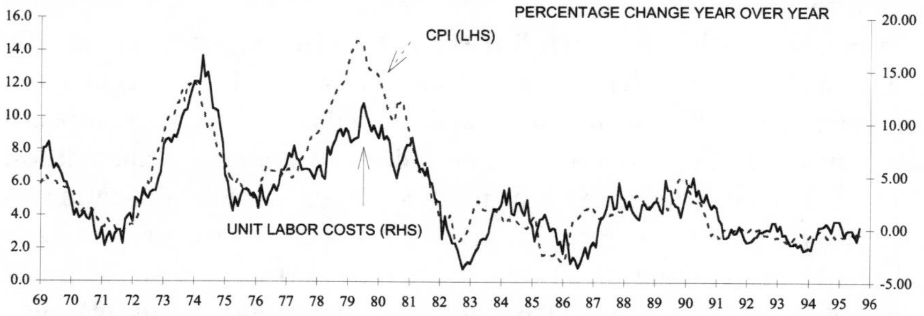

Data Source: Bureau of Labor Statistics.

costs are the major determinant of inflation within the economy. (See Exhibit 4.12.) Labor costs account for the lion's share of production costs within the U.S. economic system. Long-term trends in productivity are of interest to financial markets primarily for their impact on unit labor costs. Productivity growth is also a major driver in real GDP growth.

CORPORATE PROFITS

Quarterly, the Department of Commerce reports **Corporate Profits** in conjunction with the release of the GDP report. Profits are computed two ways: tax-based profits are derived from corporate tax returns and adjusted profits are estimated from current production.

Exhibit 4.13   Corporate Profits.

Indicator	Source	Frequency	Date & Time
Corporate Profits	Commerce Department, Bureau of Economic	Quarterly	Eight weeks after quarter end.
	Analysis		8:30 A.M. EDT

HOUSING AND CONSTRUCTION

Construction Spending includes construction outlays to build or reno-
vate residential housing, nonresidential property (e.g., office buildings
and industrial parks) and public property (e.g., highways and infrastruc-
ture). Construction spending figures are subject to long lags and major
revisions and consequently are of limited short-term value.

Financial markets tend to focus on more timely indicators such as
**Housing Starts and Building Permits; New Single-Family Home
Sales** and **Existing Home Sales.** The **Homebuilders Survey,** conducted
monthly by the National Association of Homebuilders, is widely followed and tends to be a leading indicator of new housing construction.
The linkage of the survey with new housing construction is not surpris-
ing as the survey canvasses builders' assessments of the demand for new
housing.

Housing starts and building permits are widely monitored given the
highly cyclical nature of the housing market and the sensitivity of the
sector to interest rates. Starts and permits issued, combined with sales
of existing and new homes, provide a good read on a small, albeit
volatile sector of the economy.[3]

Particular attention is paid to this sector of the economy when the
stance of monetary policy is changing or under review, or when recent
interest rate changes are being monitored to assess their effectiveness
and their impact on economic activity. **Mortgage applications** are also
monitored as yet another indicator for this sector. Applications are important primarily because of their timeliness.

INTERNATIONAL ACCOUNTS

Merchandise Trade numbers are published monthly by the Department
of Commerce, along with detailed information on imports and exports
on both a volume and a value basis. The focus tends to be on changes
in the trade balance, both monthly and on a trend basis. Considerable

---

[3] Residential construction expenditures accounted for 4.0 percent of GDP in 1996.

Exhibit 4.14   Housing and Construction.

Indicator	Source	Frequency	Date & Time
Construction Spending	Commerce Department, Bureau of the Census	Monthly	Four to five weeks after month end. 10:00 A.M. EDT
Housing Starts and Building Permits	Commerce Department, Bureau of the Census	Monthly	Two to three weeks after month end. 8:30 A.M. EDT
New Single-Family Home Sales	National Association of Realtors	Monthly	Four weeks after month end. 10:00 A.M. EDT
Homebuilders Survey	National Association of Homebuilders	Monthly	Mid-month.
Mortgage Applications	Mortgage Bankers Association	Weekly	Thursday. 8:30 A.M. EDT

attention is often given to bilateral balances with countries such as Japan and China.

Changes in the trade balance often indicate relative growth differentials between the United States and its trading partners. Strong import growth and a deteriorating trade balance indicate stronger demand in the United States than in the trading partner, and strong export demand and an improving trade balance can mean a slowdown in the domestic economy relative to the trading partners. Significant changes in the trade-weighted index of the dollar can also influence the trade balance, albeit with lags of 18 months and more. Exports account for roughly 11 percent of GDP, and imports account for about 12.5 percent of GDP.

Large swings in the monthly trade numbers can have a major impact on foreign exchange markets and thus, have important implications for international investments.

The **Current Account** component of the balance of payments includes the trade and services accounts. This report also includes investment income on direct and portfolio investments, and unilateral transfers. Release of the current account data is basically a nonevent for

Exhibit 4.15   International Accounts.

Indicator	Source	Frequency	Date & Time
Merchandise Trade	Commerce Department, Bureau of the Census	Monthly	Six to seven weeks after month end. 8:30 A.M. EDT
Current Account	Commerce Department, Bureau of Economic Analysis	Quarterly	Ten to eleven weeks after quarter end. 10:00 A.M. EDT
Capital Account	Commerce Department, Bureau of Economic Analysis	Quarterly	Ten to eleven weeks after quarter end. 10:00 A.M. EDT

financial markets. The important data are already available in the monthly trade data or elsewhere.

The **Capital Account,** the offset to the current account, provides a breakdown on capital flows. Partial data on capital flows are available from other sources, including the U.S. Treasury Department. The capital account data are too dated to be of serious relevance for financial markets.

MONETARY AND CREDIT AGGREGATES

In the eighties, financial markets lived and died by the **Monetary Aggregates** (base money, M1, M2 and M3), when the linkages between the aggregates and nominal GDP growth were defined and measurable. As these linkages have broken down, the focus on the aggregates has diminished dramatically. The Fed continues to set targets for M2 and M3 (the broader aggregates), but little attention is paid to these targets by the Fed or by financial markets.

M1 consists of the most liquid financial instruments and includes currency and demand deposits. M2 includes M1 plus savings deposit, time deposits and retail money market mutual funds. M3 includes M2 and overnight repurchase agreements, overnight Eurodollar deposits and broker/dealer money market funds.

Exhibit 4.16   Monetary and Credit Aggregates.

Indicator	Source	Frequency	Date & Time
Monetary Aggregates (M1, M2 & M3)	Federal Reserve Board	Weekly	Every Thursday. 4:30 P.M. EDT

FEDERAL GOVERNMENT FINANCES

Financial markets, particularly fixed-income markets, are keenly interested in fiscal conditions and tend to focus on the trend of the **federal deficit** and the **deficit and federal debt as a percent of GDP.** Particular attention is paid to the U.S. situation relative to other countries. Occasionally, economists and financial market practitioners will focus on the structural deficit, which eliminates cyclical influences—a particularly relevant factor when evaluating some of the European countries' fiscal positions.

Financial markets also focus on the **U.S. Treasury's borrowing schedule,** which is widely publicized in advance. Quarterly refunding of the major maturities, for example, 10- and 30-year bonds is done on a predictable cycle each quarter. These refundings tend to be closely monitored by market practitioners.

Federal Budget Balance figures are released monthly. These figures are quite volatile and not seasonally adjusted. Most economists evaluate them by comparing them to figures for the same month during the previous year.

Exhibit 4.17   Federal Government Finances.

Indicator	Source	Frequency	Date & Time
Federal Budget Balance	Treasury Department, Financial Management Service	Monthly	Fifteenth business day of the month. 2:00 P.M. EDT

SELECTED REFERENCES

Internet Economic Indicator Web Sites

There are numerous web sites that are useful sources for information on key economic indicators. The White House maintains an economic statistics briefing room www.whitehouse.govt/fsbr/esbr that contains data and graphs on the latest indicators. Each indicator is linked via a hot link back to the producing agency site for additional detail. Ed Yardeni, the Chief Economist for Deutsche Morgan Grenfell, maintains an extensive site at www.yardeni.com. The site contains data, graphs, analysis and commentary. The Bureau of Economic Analysis home page is www.bea.doc.gov/. The Census bureau site is www.census.gov/. The Bureau of Labor Statistics has an excellent site at www.stats.bls .gov/. The Conference Board site is www.conference–board.org and www.tcb-indicators.org for the leading economic indicators. The Federal Reserve site is www.bog.frb.fed.us/. The Federal Reserve Bank of Philadelphia is at pma.libertynet.org:81/fedresrv/econ/bos and the Federal Reserve Bank of Atlanta is at www.brbatlanta.org. Treasuries public debt site is www.publicdebt.treas.gov and the general site is www.ustreas.gov/. The National Association of Purchasing Managers site is www.napm.org/rob. The Commodity research bureau site is news.bridge.com/crb/crbindex.

Economic Report of the President, Council of Economic Advisers. Washington, DC: U.S. Government Printing Office, 1997.

Giordano, Robert, and Youngdahl, John. *Understanding U.S. Economic Statistics,* 2nd Ed. Economic Research, New York: Goldman Sachs.

Kuwayama, Patricia, and O'Sullivan, James. *Global Data Watch Handbook.* New York: JP Morgan, January 1996.

Niemira, Michael P., and Zukowski, Gerald F. *Trading the Fundamentals.* Chicago: Probus Publishing Co., 1994.

"Notes on Current Labor Statistics," *Monthly Labor Review.* Washington, DC: U.S. Department of Labor, June 1996.

Survey of Current Business. Washington, DC: U.S. Department of Commerce, Bureau of Economic Analysis. Various issues.

Appendix 4.1   Cyclical Indicators.

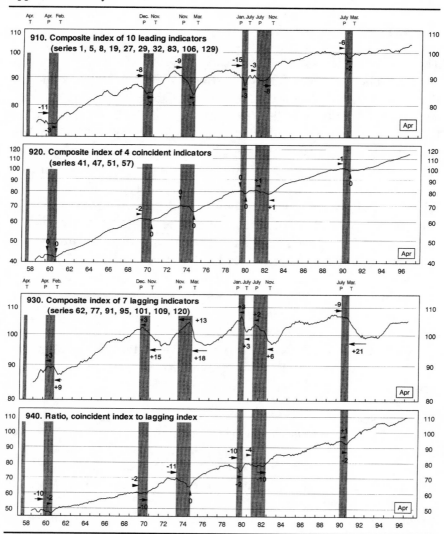

Composite Indexes

Index: 1992 = 100

Note: Series 910, 920, 930, and 940 are plotted on a ratio scale.

Appendix 4.1 *(Continued)*

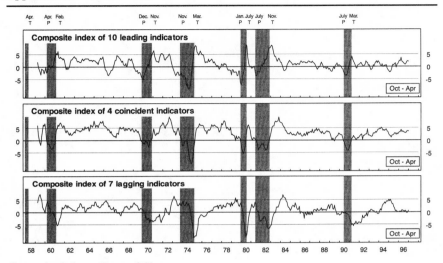

Composite Indexes: Rates of Change

Percent change over 6-month span, annual rate

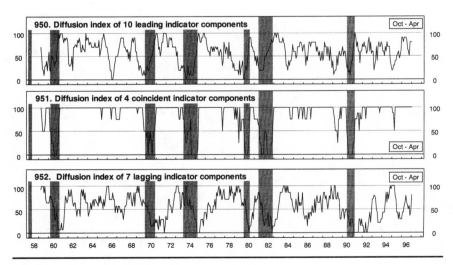

Composite Indexes: Diffusion

Percent of components rising over 6-month span

Data Source: "Business Cycle Indicators," The Conference Board, Volume 2, Number 6, p. 5 & 6, June 1997, New York.

5   The Stock Market and the Business Cycle

STOCK MARKET RETURNS AND THE GROWTH CYCLE

The performance of the U.S. stock market reflects myriad factors ranging from economic fundamentals to corporate strategies and investor psychology. Generalizations about the behavior of the market and the influence of economic fundamentals on stock performance are fraught with difficulty. Nevertheless, useful observations and generalizations can be made because the market reflects the aggregate behavior of a substantial portion of the productive economy.

As all market participants know, the stock market is acutely sensitive to the growth and monetary policy cycles. A matrix of economic and interest rate environments is set out in Exhibit 5.1 to describe the performance of the stock market under various conditions. The growth cycle is characterized by four different environments. Growth above or below trend is broken down into growth that either converges on the trend output level or diverges and moves further away from the trend output level. For example, an increasing positive output gap reflects a period when the economy was already operating above its long-term trend growth potential, and growth in the current period is advancing above the level registered in the previous period. The four growth environments are further broken down into periods when short-term interest rates were either rising or falling. The rationale for breaking down the growth profile in this way is the critical importance of interest rate movements and their impact on the stock market.

Exhibit 5.1   Stock Market Returns, the Growth Cycle and Monetary Policy.

January 1979 to December 1995
(Standard deviation of returns in parentheses)

	Phase I	Phase II	Phase III	Phase IV
	Negative & Decreasing/ Narrowing Output Gap	Positive & Increasing/ Widening Output Gap	Positive & Decreasing/ Narrowing Output Gap	Negative & Increasing/ Widening Output Gap
Increasing Short-Term Interest Rates				
Total Return	7.3 %	5.9 %	16.2 %	4.1 %
Standard Deviation	(3.2)%	(4.9)%	(4.6)%	(2.9)%
Excess Return	−0.5 %	−1.7 %	6.5 %	−4.7 %
Standard Deviation	(3.1)%	(5.7)%	(4.8)%	(3.1)%
Monthly Observations	23	42	25	7
Decreasing Short-Term Interest Rates				
Total Return	17.9 %	28.7 %	12.8 %	32.3 %
Standard Deviation	(2.7)%	(3.9)%	(4.7)%	(4.4)%
Excess Return	12.6 %	19.5 %	4.1 %	23.2 %
Standard Deviation	(2.6)%	(3.9)%	(4.7)%	(4.4)%
Monthly Observations	16	27	32	32

Methodology: Monthly total returns for each period of the growth cycle were chain-lined to compute an annualized geometric return for each phase. This approach permits reasonable comparison across various economic environments. Excess returns are returns above three-month Treasury bills. Ninety-day Treasury bill yields were used for the measure of short-term interest rates. The interest rate environment is determined by the direction of change in short-term interest rates over the three month period. An increasing output gap is a gap that is moving further away from potential; a decreasing output gap is a gap that is moving in the direction of potential.

Total returns are based on total returns for the S&P 500 Index.

Data Source: Datastream.

Negative Output Gaps and Stock Market Returns

The stock market registered the best performance over the 17-year period from 1979 through 1995 when the economy was operating below potential and short-term interest rates were decreasing. (See Exhibit 5.1.) During the 48 months when the economy was growing below potential and interest rates were decreasing (Phases I and IV, combined, lower panel), the market returned an annualized 27.3 percent and an annualized excess return of 19.5 percent. The 32 months when the economy was operating below potential and deteriorating (Phase IV, lower panel) were even more rewarding: The market returned 32.3 percent on an annualized basis. These returns were generated primarily during the months immediately preceding and following the troughs of the recessions of 1981–1982 and 1990–1991. Recovery from the nine-month recession of 1990–1991 was slow. The output gap continued to expand for nine months after the trough of the recession. During this period, market returns were positive but volatile. It should be pointed out that the early phases of a recession can be brutal, but sharp early declines are generally followed by a relaxation of monetary policy and anticipation that an economic upturn will subsequently support the market.

Periods during which the output gap was negative and interest rates were increasing (Phases I and IV, upper panel, Exhibit 5.1) occurred primarily following major recessions. The economy had bottomed, excess capacity was rapidly diminishing and the Fed was tightening monetary policy on a forward-looking basis. In the face of these interest rate head winds, the market registered only modest gains and actually underperformed cash.

The stock market is a leading indicator of the economy and, like other leading indicators, it tends to foreshadow a downturn 9 to 18 months in advance of a peak in economic activity. Historically, the market has peaked before an economic downturn. The recessions of 1980, 1981–1982 and 1990–1991, on the other hand, did not have a market peak prior to the downturn in the economy. Instead, the market peaked at the beginning of the downturn. The early phase of a recession is a particularly brutal time for stocks with the market selling off sharply. About 4 to 6 months prior to the trough of a recession, the stock market begins a very strong recovery, which generally accelerates through the trough of the business cycle. This is the optimal time to buy stocks.

Positive Output Gaps and Stock Market Returns

When the economy is operating above potential—that is, with a positive output gap—and interest rates are increasing, it is extremely difficult for the market to make much headway. During the 17-year period from 1979 to 1995, there were 67 months in which the economy grew above trend and interest rates increased (Phases II and III, upper panel,

Exhibit 5.1). Market returns averaged only 9.6 percent on an annualized basis, and a scant 1.1 percent above the return on cash.

During periods when the economy has been operating above potential and accelerating and the Fed has been increasing interest rates (Phase II, upper panel), the market has performed very poorly. The annualized return was a meager 5.9 percent or −1.7 percent below cash. In part, returns in this environment were low because the time span under consideration includes the stock market crash of October 1987, which saw an increase in short-term interest rates of 168 basis points in the three months before the crash, and the economy growing almost 2 percent above trend. While excluding October 1987—the month of the crash— as a major single event might seem appropriate, it would be significant only if the sharp run-up in the market during the months immediately prior to the crash were excluded, along with the recovery of the market in December, January and February. This would, however, be a selective after-the-fact adjustment in the data which, on reflection, does not seem warranted.

The second best market returns have been achieved during periods when the economy has operated above potential, with the output gap increasing but with short-term interest rates decreasing (Phase II, lower panel). During the 27 months when this environment prevailed, the market registered gains of 28.7 percent and excess returns of 19.5 percent. Over the entire period of 59 months when the economy was operating above potential but with a constructive interest rate environment (Phase II and III, lower panel), the market registered gains of 19.8 percent on an annualized basis. This environment is perfect for stocks. The economy is operating at or near full capacity with high corporate profit margins and inflation remains contained to a point where the Federal Reserve can ease short-term interest rates.

PRICE VERSUS DIVIDEND RETURNS

Over the 17-year period from January 1979 through December 1995, the S&P 500 registered compound annual total returns of 16.5 percent, with 12.5 percent registered as price appreciation. That is, 75.6 percent

Exhibit 5.2   S&P 500 Price Performance.

Year	S&P	Year	S&P	Year	S&P	Year	S&P	Year	S&P
1945	30.7 %	1955	26.4 %	1965	9.1 %	1975	31.6 %	1985	26.3 %
1946	(11.9)	1956	2.6	1966	(13.1)	1976	19.2	1986	14.6
1947	0.0	1957	(14.3)	1967	20.1	1977	(11.5)	1987	2.0
1948	(0.7)	1958	38.1	1968	7.7	1978	1.1	1988	12.4
1949	10.3	1959	8.5	1969	11.4	1979	12.3	1989	27.3
1950	21.8	1960	(3.0)	1970	0.1	1980	25.8	1990	(6.6)
1951	16.5	1961	23.1	1971	10.8	1981	(9.7)	1991	26.3
1952	11.8	1962	(11.8)	1972	15.6	1982	14.8	1992	4.5
1953	(6.6)	1963	18.9	1973	(17.4)	1983	17.3	1993	7.1
1954	45.0	1964	13.0	1974	(29.7)	1984	1.4	1994	(1.5)
								1995	34.1

Data Source: Datastream.

of the return to the S&P 500 was price appreciation and 24.4 percent was dividend income. Exhibit 5.2 gives the annual price appreciation of the S&P 500 since the end of World War II.

Although there are some substantial down years, the dividend yield would have helped to ameliorate the impact of price depreciation.

Exhibit 5.3 depicts the S&P 500 rolling 12-month total returns from 1980 to 1996. The attractiveness of equities is clearly evident, given the generally strong returns over most 12-month periods.

Exhibit 5.3   S&P 500 Rolling 12-Month Total Returns.

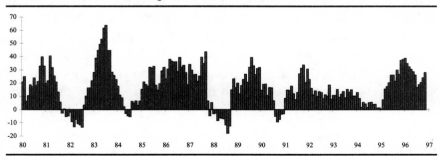

Data Source: Datastream.

IMPACT OF THE BUSINESS CYCLE ON CORPORATE EARNINGS AND PROFITS

Corporate earnings are the driving force behind the stock market. They constitute the link between the real economy and the market. Investors in the stock market are, in effect, purchasing an interest in the future stream of corporate earnings which are, in aggregate, driven by the growth and performance of the economy. The long-term secular trend of the economy and the progression of the economy through the business cycle set the level and growth of earnings and profits at any given point.

Corporate Profits and Economic Growth

Over time, corporate earnings and profits tend to grow in line with the economy. As shown in Exhibit 5.4, over the 35-year period from 1960 to 1995, real and nominal profit growth roughly matched real and nominal GNP growth.[1] Nominal profits grew at an average annual rate of 8.2 percent relative to nominal GNP growth of 7.7 percent, and real profits grew by 3.7 percent relative to real GNP growth of 3.2 percent. Over shorter time periods, however, the divergence between economic growth and profit growth has often been substantial—due in large measure to changes in profits' share of GNP.

Profits' share of GNP varied over the 35-year period from 1960 to 1995. (See Exhibit 5.5.) The range went from a low of 4.9 percent in 1982 (a year of severe recession) to a high of 11.2 percent in 1965. Changes in the percentage of economic income accruing to profits will result in changes in the relative growth of profits and GNP. All else being equal, a declining share will produce profit growth that lags economic growth and an increasing share will yield profit growth that outpaces economic growth.

Recessionary periods tend to feature an erosion of profits' share of GNP. When the economy slips into recession, corporations respond by

---

[1] GNP is used as the broad measure of the economy because it includes foreign-factor income payments and receipts, which are also reflected in corporate profits.

Exhibit 5.4 Corporate Profits and Economic Growth.

| | Nominal | | Real | | Corporate |
| | Average Profit Growth | Average GNP Growth | Average Profit Growth | Average GNP Growth | Profits as a Percent of |
Period					GNP
1960–1995	8.2	7.7	3.7	3.2	7.8
1976–1995	9.3	7.8	4.4	2.8	6.8
1986–1995	6.8	5.6	3.6	2.4	6.8
1991–1995	11.3	4.8	8.3	1.9	7.1

Average annual growth. Nonfinancial corporate profits with inventory valuation and capital consumption adjustments. Nominal profits deflated by the GNP deflator.

Data Source: U.S. Commerce Department, Bureau of Economic Analysis.

cutting production. Their ability to rationalize production is limited by fixed costs and by efforts to maintain production above critical break-even levels. In this environment, profits are quickly eroded. Economy-wide excess capacity reduces pricing power—and, ultimately, profits. Resumption of growth generally results in a restoration of profits' share of GNP.

Profits' share of GNP also tends to be eroded during periods of sharply accelerating inflation, as were experienced during the Vietnam War and the two oil-shock episodes of the seventies. Consumers respond with considerable resistance to an immediate and full pass-through of costs, and the typical results are a squeeze on margins and erosion of

Exhibit 5.5 Profits' Share of GNP.

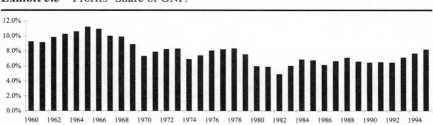

Data Source: Bureau of Economic Analysis.

profit.[2] Conversely, a marked deceleration of inflation will bring a restoration of profits' share of GNP.

Changes in profits' share of GNP can have a powerful leveraging effect on profit growth. For example, profits accounted for 6.4 percent of GNP in 1992, and then increased to 8.1 percent of GNP in 1995.[3] This increase brought explosive growth of profits during the period, above and beyond what would have occurred had the share remained constant.

Costs and Profit per Unit of Output

On a unit-of-output basis, employee compensation, which generally comprises two-thirds of costs, is the major cost faced by corporations. Compensation tends to be heavily influenced by inflation and unit labor costs closely track the consumer price index (CPI) (see Exhibit 5.13, on page 81). For example, during the high inflation year of 1974, employee compensation took up 68.5 percent of corporate revenue. In 1995, when inflation was only 2.8 percent, employee compensation comprised only 65.9 percent of total costs. Indirect business taxes generally have accounted for around 10 percent of costs on a unit-of-output basis. The incidence of taxes on corporate profits are quite variable, depending on the legislated corporate tax rates and corporate profits. For large corporations, the average tax rate is 34 percent of taxable income.[4] Depreciation and net interest charges take up the remainder of corporate costs. Net interest expenses are highly variable, depending on the level of inflation and interest rates in the economy. Profits are therefore a highly volatile residual, and have ranged (on a unit-of-output basis) from a high of 17.3 percent to a low of 6.4 percent since 1960.

Five "snapshots" of corporate America's cost structure under different economic conditions are presented in Exhibit 5.6.

---

[2] A full pass-through of unit labor costs takes up to 2 years. See note 7 in this chapter.
[3] Corporate profits with inventory valuation and capital consumption adjustments.
[4] Tax Reform Act of 1986.

Exhibit 5.6   Costs and Profit per Unit of Output.*

	Total Cost & Profits	Depreciation	Indirect Business Taxes	Compensation of Employees	Corporate Profits with Inventory Valuation and Capital Consumption Adjustments			Net Interest
					Total	Tax	Profits after Tax	
1965	100.0	8.5	10.1	62.5	17.3	6.8	10.4	1.6
1974	100.0	9.6	10.1	68.5	8.5	5.3	3.3	3.5
1982	100.0	12.9	9.5	66.7	6.4	2.5	3.8	4.5
1989	100.0	11.4	9.5	66.1	8.1	3.3	4.7	5.0
1995	100.0	10.9	10.2	65.9	10.3	3.6	6.7	2.6

* Per unit GDP of nonfinancial corporate businesses in current dollars.
Data Source: Department of Commerce, Bureau of Economic Analysis.

Corporate Profits and the Business Cycle

The relationship of the corporate profit cycle and the business cycle is presented in Exhibit 5.7. On average, over the 41 years from the IV quarter of 1949 to the III quarter of 1990, corporate profits declined an average of 20.0 percent from peak to trough in nine profit cycles and rose an average of 31.5 percent in the immediate recovery phases following the profit troughs.

The pattern of corporate profits identified in Exhibit 5.7 supports the overall performance of the stock market presented earlier. Profits, like the stock market, recover roughly one quarter prior to the trough of the business cycle, and grow very strongly during the initial phase of economic recovery. Profits also peak before or coincident with the peak in the business cycle with the longest lead time being 7 quarters diminishing down to no lead at all prior to the peak in economic activity.

Industrial Production, Capacity Utilization, Fixed Costs, Productivity and Unit Labor Costs

Industrial production and capacity utilization are two key indicators and guideposts for monitoring swings in corporate profits through the

Exhibit 5.7   Profits and the Business Cycle.

Profit Trough	Percent Decline Peak to Trough	Duration of Decline (Quarters)	Profit Lead at Business Cycle Peak	Percent Rise in Burst Phase of Rebound	Duration of Burst (Quarters)	Profit Lead at Business Cycle Trough
1949 IVQ	−18.0	4	0	56.5	4	1
1953 IVQ	−22.7	8	7	27.7	4	3
1958 IQ	−23.9	9	7	29.7	4	1
1961 IQ	−17.4	7	4	28.7	4	0
1970 IVQ	−21.5	8	4	34.0	5	0
1974 IVQ	−16.7	7	3	55.6	5	1
1980 IIQ	−27.2	6	5	22.8	3	1
1982 IQ	−27.0	2	0	16.0	2	3
1990 IIIQ	−10.8	1	0	12.3	2	0
Average	−20.0	5.8	3.3	31.5	3.7	1.1

Data Source: Jill Jacobs, "Profits and Labor, the Pendulum at Rest," *Economic Research,* Goldman Sachs, June 1996.

business cycle. Year-on-year peaks in industrial production growth generally occur contemporaneously with peaks in nonfinancial corporate profits (see Exhibit 5.9). Capacity utilization levels tend to peak roughly contemporaneously with, or several quarters after, corporate profits' peak.

Exhibit 5.8   Corporate Profits (Annual Percentage Change).

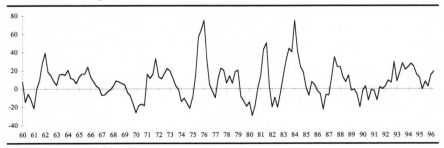

Data Source: Bureau of Economic Analysis.

Exhibit 5.9   Industrial Production and Corporate Profits.

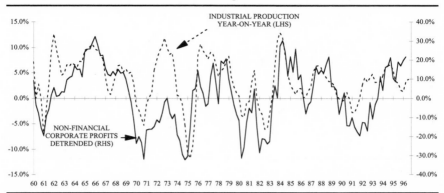

Data Source: Bureau of Economic Analysis and the Federal Reserve Board.

Given the high level of fixed costs corporations must bear, any change in activity results in an immediate decrease or increase in earnings and profits as average costs adjust. In fact, the correlation between manufacturing capacity utilization—which serves as a proxy for fixed costs—and nonfinancial corporate profits is high, as Exhibit 5.10 indicates.[5]

As spare capacity—both capital and labor—is utilized, corporate profitability increases substantially. Capacity constraints then begin to emerge and exert higher marginal costs on corporations. This is clearly evident from Exhibit 5.11 below which shows the relationship between the GDP output gap—actual output vs. potential output—and swings in corporate profits. The correlation between the output gap and deviations from trend earnings is strong.

When dealing with fixed capital constraints, corporations either increase capital utilization (through, for example, multiple shifts) or begin to add capacity through business fixed investment. There is a very tight link between capacity utilization rates and changes in gross private fixed investment (see Exhibit 5.12).

---

[5] Nonfinancial corporate profits adjusted for inventory valuations and capital consumption. Inventories are adjusted for inflation and capital depreciation is standardized to straight-line depreciation.

Exhibit 5.10   Capacity Utilization Rates and Corporate Profits.

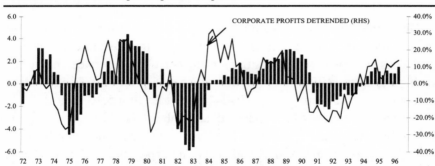

Data Source: Bureau of Economic Analysis and the Federal Reserve Board.

Exhibit 5.11   U.S. Output Gap and Corporate Profits.

Data Source: Bureau of Economic Analysis.

Exhibit 5.12   Business Fixed Investment and the Capacity Utilization Rate.

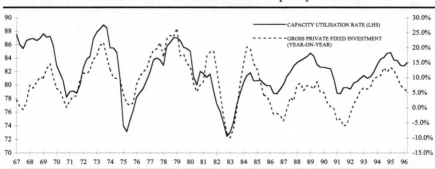

Data Source: Bureau of Economic Analysis and the Federal Reserve Board.

Exhibit 5.13   Employment Cost Index and the CPI.

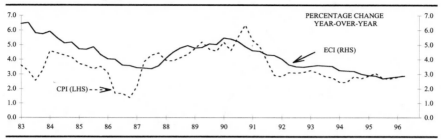

Data Source: Bureau of Labor Statistics.

Often, the most pressing constraint is skilled labor. Shortages in the labor market ultimately lead to increased compensation costs and higher unit labor costs.[6] Labor costs are the principal cost borne by corporations. As stated previously, they constitute about two-thirds of the average business's expenses (see Exhibit 5.13).

After the economy has reached operating capacity and constraints begin to emerge, profit gains become contingent on sales expansion through increases in market share, productivity gains, or the existence of pricing power, so that corporations can pass on rising costs to customers. To the extent these options are blocked or constrained, earnings and profit margins are inevitably squeezed.

During the final stage of a business expansion, corporations typically possess considerable pricing power, given the lack of excess capacity in the system and the emergence of inflationary pressure generally within the economy.[7] Inevitably, however, this pricing power

---

[6] Several good measures of labor costs are worth monitoring. The most important and comprehensive measure, from the perspective of corporations, is *unit labor costs,* which are available quarterly and measure labor cost per unit of output. This measure's overriding advantage is that it incorporates changes in productivity. The employment cost index (ECI) measures total compensation—wages and benefits. This index is standardized by occupation and is not affected by shifts in type of work. The most timely measure of employment costs is the average hourly earnings figures contained in the monthly employment report generated by the Department of Labor. Unfortunately, this index suffers from several shortcomings, including sensitivity to shifts in the type of work and to overtime. Nevertheless, it is timely and therefore is useful.

[7] Economists at Goldman Sachs estimate that 100 percent of unit labor costs are passed through to the CPI within 2 years, with 75 percent of this pass-through occurring during the first year. *U.S. Economic Analyst,* Goldman Sachs, April 26, 1996.

Exhibit 5.14   Unit Labor Costs and the CPI.

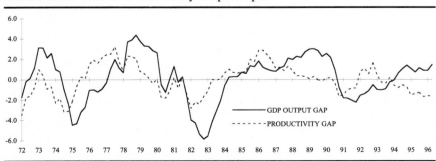

Data Source: Bureau of Labor Statistics.

exacerbates inflationary pressures and forces an offsetting adjustment of monetary policy (Exhibit 5.14). There is some anecdotal evidence to suggest that corporate pricing power is increasingly circumscribed by global competition.

Productivity growth is a major contributor to real GDP and profit growth. From 1972 to mid-1996, trend productivity growth—as measured by output per hour—was 1.25 percent. Deviations around this trend are significant as Exhibit 5.15 shows. The gaps or deviations from the horizontal axis indicate deviations from trend GDP and productivity growth. Swings in productivity growth around trend are driven by both the output gap and changes in growth. That is, productivity generally

Exhibit 5.15   GDP and Productivity Output Gaps.

Data Source: Bureau of Economic Analysis and Bureau of Labor Statistics.

grows *above trend* when the output gap is positive and *below trend* when the output gap is negative.

Compounding the problem of employment cost pressure late in the cycle is the deceleration of productivity growth as the expansion matures. Incremental gains in productivity diminish as the factors of production—particularly fixed capacity such as plant and equipment—are more fully utilized. Late in the cycle, corporations are generally forced to employ increasingly marginal factors of production (both labor and capital), thus diminishing average output per worker. This is evident in Exhibit 5.15 which relates the output and productivity gaps.[8]

Productivity tends to peak well before output and to trough before output troughs. During an expansion, the marginal productivity of both capital and labor begins to diminish as capacity within the economy is increasingly utilized. The addition of marginal factors of production diminishes average factor productivity as capacity becomes tight. As the economy turns down, labor is laid off, leaving plant and equipment idle, reducing average productivity.[9]

In terms of the business cycle, productivity peaks roughly two quarters before the peak in economic activity. The downturn in productivity has averaged −1.1 percent prior to the peak in activity during the past six business cycles. Total productivity declines during the past six recessions have averaged −2.3 percent (see Exhibit 5.16).

The decline in productivity at the end of the expansion phase of the business cycle equates to a decline in profit margins because the decline in productivity effectively translates into a rise in unit labor costs. With labor costs comprising roughly two-thirds of total cost, the levered impact is quite significant.

The decline in productivity at the end of the cycle works in tandem with the increase in unit labor costs and precipitates an upward spiral of prices, a compression of margins and an earnings squeeze.

---

[8] The output gap is derived from the residuals generated from regressing the log of real GDP. The productivity gap is derived in the same manner. Productivity is measured using the Department of Labor's output-per-hour data.

[9] The output gap is cumulative through time; it is a measure of the cumulative deviation from trend. Thus, for example, if the economy emerges from a recession but growth is initially below trend, the output gap will continue to expand even though the economy is experiencing positive growth.

Exhibit 5.16   Productivity and the Business Cycle.

Recessions	Productivity Lead at Cycle Peak	Percent Decline Prior to GDP Peak	Total Productivity Decline Peak/Trough
IIQ 1960 to IQ 1961	1	−1.6	−2.5
IVQ 1969 to IVQ 1970	3	−1.0	−1.4
IVQ 1973 to IQ 1975	3	−1.0	−3.1
IQ 1980 to IIIQ 1980	5	−1.9	−2.9
IIIQ 1981 to IVQ 1982	2	−1.1	−2.5
IIQ 1990 to IQ 1991	0	0.0	−1.2
Average	2.3	−1.1	−2.3

Data Source: Jill Jacobs, "Winds at the Back of Corporate Profits," *U.S. Economic Analyst,* Issue No. 96/38, Goldman Sachs, September 20, 1996.

INVENTORIES, MONETARY POLICY AND CORPORATE PROFITS

Inventory Cycle

The two leading causes of recessions are: inventory cycle corrections and/or interest rate increases precipitated by inflation. As economic growth weakens, involuntary inventory accumulation often occurs because production has been slow to adjust to changing demand. This inventory accumulation prompts production cuts and further slowing of the economy. Ultimately, production adjustments lead to inventory rundowns and restoration of a lean or normal inventory–sales ratio. At this point, growth troughs and voluntary inventory accumulation resume in anticipation of improving sales.

The historic relationship between inventory changes and changes in industrial production are depicted in Exhibit 5.17. The leads and lags in inventory adjustment and industrial production adjustment are pronounced. The key to deciphering the state of play, at any given point in the cycle, is an assessment of whether the inventory changes are voluntary or involuntary. Sales patterns, discounting and incentive programs often (but not always) provide useful insights into the inventory picture.

Exhibit 5.17   Business Inventories and Industrial Production.

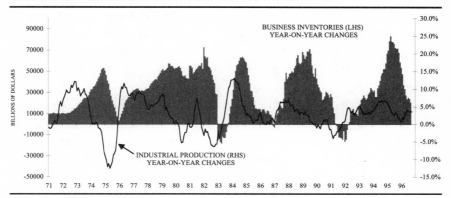

Data Source: Bureau of Economic Analysis and the Federal Reserve Board.

Inventory imbalances are a major factor contributing to sharp swings in economic growth. Historically, the inventory cycle has exacerbated every growth cycle since World War II and has been evident in every recession.

The introduction of just-in-time inventory management may, over time, moderate the magnitude of inventory imbalances, but it has also made the inventory cycle somewhat more volatile because production responds very quickly to inventory imbalances. Volatility may have increased, but the magnitude of inventory swings may have moderated.

Given the link between inventories and industrial production, it is not difficult to appreciate the importance of inventories during the business and profit cycle.

The Stock Market and the Monetary Policy Cycle

The inventory cycle is often exacerbated by the monetary cycle. Declining growth often prompts the Federal Reserve to adopt an accommodative monetary stance and lower interest rates. Often, interest rate cuts continue even after the economy registers initial signs of a recovery. This creates an ideal environment for stocks. Earnings and profits are increasing because of an improvement in growth as the inventory

correction cycle concludes. Excess liquidity, prompted by loose monetary policy, floods into financial assets, as attractive investments in real
assets, such as plant and equipment, is limited in the early part of the
upturn due to the existence of substantial excess capacity. This liquidity is a major driver of share prices in the early stages of a market's recovery.

Interest-sensitive sectors of the economy—such as housing and long-
term business fixed investment—begin to recover under the auspices of
cheap money. This progresses until accelerating activity prompts constraints and inflation. Tightening ensues, the economy slows and the
cycle is repeated.

IMPACT OF INTEREST RATES ON THE STOCK MARKET

Not only do interest rates play a major role in the course of the business
cycle, they also significantly influence corporate costs, stock valuations
and the attractiveness of equities relative to cash and bonds.

Corporate Interest Expenses

Interest rates affect corporate costs because interest is a key expense for
corporations. In fact, interest expenses are among the most volatile cost
components faced by corporations (see Exhibit 5.6).

Valuation Adjustments

Standard financial theory and practice dictate that firms should be val-
ued on the discounted cash flows that will be generated in the future. Interest rates play a critical role in determining the appropriate discount
rate to apply in this process. In essence, interest rates set the base for determining the appropriate discount rate. That is, an investor would expect to receive a return at least equal to the return on a default or
risk-free U.S. Treasury bond when investing in a company or portfolio
of companies. Market participants and practitioners often use the yield

on 30-year U.S. Treasury bonds as the base for discounting earnings.[10] They then gross-up the expected Treasury bond yield by an appropriate risk premium, which takes into account the added risk of equities in general, and by an additional factor to cover specific company or portfolio risk.

All other things being equal, higher interest rates result in a higher discount factor, which reduces the value of future earnings and therefore the firm's market price. Lower interest rates increase the value of the firm. A high discount factor reduces the value of future cash flow receipts while a low discount factor increases the value.

Equities Relative to Alternative Investments

Interest rates impact the stock market by establishing the level of expected returns for alternate investments. Specifically, interest rates reflect the return on cash and on cash-like investments, and the expected return from the bond market. Both cash and bond investments are low-risk alternatives to equity investments. They play an important role in investors' decisions to invest in equities or lower-risk alternatives.

SELECTED REFERENCES

Jacobs, Jill. "Profits and Labor, the Pendulum at Rest," *Economic Research,* Goldman Sachs, June 1996.

Jacobs, Jill. "Winds at the Back of Corporate Profits," *U.S. Economic Analyst,* Issue No. 96/38 Goldman Sachs, September 20, 1996.

---

[10] Thirty-year Treasury bonds are used because they are long-dated instruments with a duration comparable to the foreseeable horizon for a corporation.

6 Sector Rotation within the Stock Market

Sector rotation—the process or strategy of rotating a stock portfolio through time in order to concentrate on specific market sectors or industries and take advantage of changes in relative performance—is one of the most important decisions an investor makes. Timely sector rotation has the potential to add significantly more to returns than stock selection. Indeed, a substantial portion of individual stock performance results from both overall market performance and sector and industry performance. The relationship of the business cycle to the stock market cycle, and the periods when various categories of stocks experience relative outperformance is depicted in Exhibit 6.1.

Exhibit 6.2, which shows the ten best and ten worst performing industry groups within the S&P 500 from June 1995 to June 1996, illustrates the value of timely sector rotation. The spread between the best and worst performing industries was 102.7 percent. The strongest industry outperformed the broad market index by 65.1 percent over the one-year period, and the weakest industry lagged the index by 37.6 percent.

According to Salomon Brothers, the quarterly spread between the highest and lowest industry quintiles in the S&P 500 was generally greater than 20 percent over the 9-year period from 1986 through 1994, and sometimes exceeded 30 percent in a single quarter.[1] Unquestionably, accurate sector timing can add significantly to portfolio performance.

---

[1] Eric Sorensen, "Investing in Industry Groups—Top to Bottom," *Global Derivatives Review* (Salomon Brothers, New York), March 1995.

Exhibit 6.1   Sector Rotation and the Business Cycle: Optimal Investment Points.

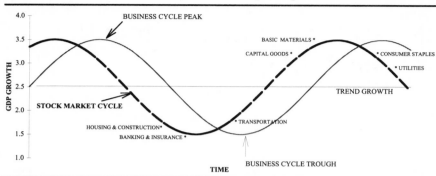

Exhibit 6.2   S&P 500 Industry Ranked Returns: Best and Worst Performing Groups (6/30/95 to 6/30/96).

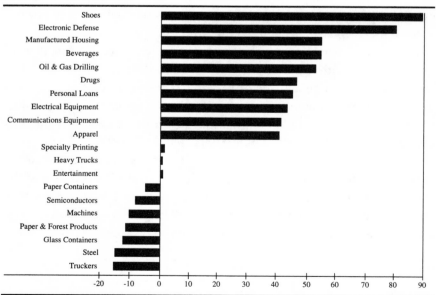

Data Source: Bloomberg.

Various industries and stock categories may perform very differently, depending on their economic environment. Some stocks benefit dramatically from a pickup in economic activity while other stocks such as food and drug companies register steady, somewhat predictable growth over the various phases of the business cycle. Other companies, such as banks, are sensitive to the interest rate environment.[2]

Appendix 6.2 reviews in detail the relative performance of sectors and industries under different economic environments since 1976.

METHODOLOGY AND FRAMEWORK[3]

A useful construct for considering sector rotation is to view each sector's price performance relative to the market as a whole which, in this instance, is the stocks contained in the S&P 500 stock index. Measuring sector and industry performance relative to the whole market filters out general market risk and permits a focus on the forces that have a unique impact on sectors and industries.

Most of the analysis that follows looks at relative sector performance on a quarterly basis against changes in quarterly GDP and other relevant economic variables. Six separate categories have been established to characterize economic conditions: (1) rising growth (the evaluated quarter's growth rate above the previous quarter's growth rate); (2) falling growth (the evaluated quarter's growth rate below the previous quarter's growth rate); (3) growth above trend and rising; (4) growth above trend and falling; (5) growth below trend and rising and (6) growth below trend and falling. (Appendix 6.2 contains the analysis of sector performance under the six categories.) The exhibits characterize growth as either rising or falling.

The rationale for using quarterly data is severalfold. The stock market is clearly forward-looking, and, in aggregate, responds in advance of

---

[2] A good discussion of some of the issues involved in sector rotation is contained in James L. Farrell, *Guide to Portfolio Management,* pp. 205–232. New York: McGraw-Hill, 1983.
[3] The analysis herein was conducted using data from June 1976 to June 1996, when available. For some sectors, particularly some of the smaller sectors, the time span is shorter with the exact time span reported in Appendix 6.2.

foreshadowed economic changes. Sectors and industries tend to be acutely sensitive to quarterly and monthly changes in economic data, and they adjust quickly to new economic "information" contained in economic data releases, which, by definition, are embedded in GDP. The adjustment of stocks and market sectors to new economic information is captured by relating contemporaneous changes in the economy with changes in the relative sector's price performance. Where appropriate, leads and lags are suggested or built into the analysis, but, by and large, changes in the economy appear to precipitate contemporaneous changes in the relative performance of industries and sectors and, as such, a contemporaneous framework was adopted.

An additional consideration when specifying the relevant time-period link between the market and the economy is the quarterly corporate earnings reporting cycle. Following the release of quarterly corporate financial information, analysts adjust their corporate earnings and growth assumptions significantly, a practice that tends to place a heavy weighting on recent experience. Also, the magnitude of potential earnings surprises decreases over time. This "bias" or focus on quarterly financial figures helps to explain, in part, the relatively contemporaneous link between sector performance and changes in the economy.

Using contemporaneous readings of sector performance and economic performance is also justifiable, given that a substantial number of major market participants focus on earnings momentum—which is significantly determined by current economic conditions—as the dominant factor in driving their investment decision making.

Numerous factors influence the performance of different industries through time. Economic conditions may exert an important influence, but secular trends and conditions can dominate for prolonged periods of time. This analysis focuses on a single dimension of a multidimensional phenomenon.

GDP GROWTH-SENSITIVE SECTORS

As all investment practitioners know, the economy, with all its vagaries, drives the stock market. In turn, some industries and sectors are significantly more sensitive to changes in economic growth than others. The GDP growth-sensitive sectors include basic and industrial materials, energy, industrial cyclicals, transportation, capital goods and consumer cyclicals. Each is examined below.

Basic and Industrial Materials

Basic and industrial materials companies, as primary and intermediate producers, benefit immediately from a pickup in economic activity given their high fixed costs and long lead times in adding new or expanded capacity. Increases in activity and material demand are generally supplied out of existing productive capacity with only marginal changes in variable costs. This improvement in asset utilization translates directly into earnings and profit growth. Moreover, as the economic cycle accelerates and excess capacity diminishes, primary and intermediate producers possess considerable pricing power given the substantial barriers to entry which include very high capital cost and long lead times required to bring new capacity on line. Cost pressures experienced by these producers can readily be passed on to final goods producers, given excess demand and the relatively small role of material prices in the overall cost equation.

Industrial materials such as iron and steel and metal mining companies are acutely sensitive to GDP growth. These sectors register their worst performance when the economy is experiencing a sharp deterioration in growth. Gold producers have experienced the strongest performance when the economy has been emerging from a slow growth period.

As Exhibit 6.3 indicates, the sensitivity of the primary material producers to changes in the economy is critical. Iron and steel in the United States has been in a secular decline for some time as low-cost producers such as Korea have increasingly gained market share at the expense of their U.S. counterparts. This explains the asymmetry of returns apparent in the exhibit. Iron and steel producers do, however, tend to modestly outperform when the economy is operating above trend and rising.

Chemical companies perform best when emerging from a recession or a severe growth slowdown. The sector often "anticipates" the

Exhibit 6.3   Basic and Industrial Materials' Relative Performance under Different Economic Conditions.

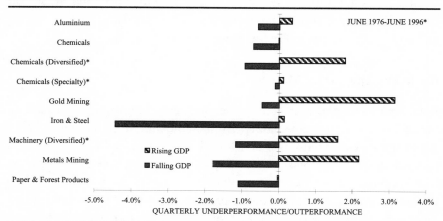

* See Appendix 6.2.

recovery by one quarter. Chemical stocks underperform during declining growth.

Paper and forest products underperformed the market 62 percent of the time during the period from June 1976 to June 1996.

The Energy Sector

The performance of energy companies relative to the broader market is directly related to changes in energy prices and, to a lesser extent, to the performance of the economy. Energy companies tend to have high operating leverage—high fixed costs and relatively low variable costs—and they benefit directly from increased demand or higher energy prices. Oil companies appear to be able to pass on price increases directly to producers and consumers alike—albeit with lags. Energy companies did particularly well during the two oil shock periods in the early and late seventies. More recently, the invasion of Kuwait by Iraq in August 1990 caused a sharp increase in the price of oil companies as oil prices spiked up. Over the past ten years, the most important variable in explaining outperformance or underperformance in the energy sector relative to

Exhibit 6.4   Oil Price Changes and the Relative Performance of the Composite Oil Price Index.

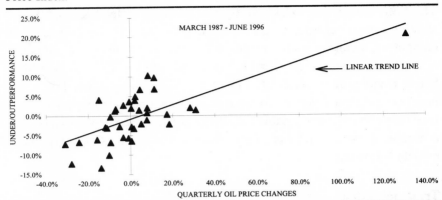

the market has been *changes* in energy prices, not the *absolute level* of energy prices (Exhibit 6.4). Significant outperformance or underperformance appears to be a price shock phenomenon. The pattern is similar for both domestic and internationally integrated oil companies and for oil and gas drilling equipment companies (Exhibit 6.5).

Natural gas producers and distributors are also sensitive to overall energy prices which benchmark off crude oil prices. To some extent, this is because gas is a substitute for oil, although long lead times and costly conversions are involved. Gas production is ancillary to oil production and is thus subject to the same influences.

Exhibit 6.5   Energy Sectors' Relative Performance under Different Economic Conditions.

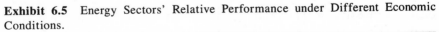
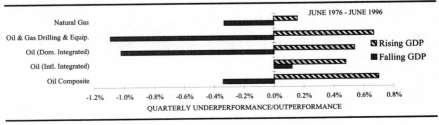

Industrial Cyclicals

The S&P industrials index closely tracks the broader S&P index and shows minimal variation as one would expect. Industrial sectors such as computers, technology, electronics, telecommunications and conglomerates are all sensitive to economic downturns when the economy dips below trend growth levels (Exhibit 6.6). These sectors perform quite poorly during mid-cycle pauses and recessions. Following a sharp downturn, however, these companies can recover before the economy resumes a normal growth trajectory. This forward-looking bias is particularly evident following severe corrections.

Transportation

As one would expect, transportation companies are quite sensitive to changes in economic activity given their high fixed capital costs and fixed capacity (Exhibit 6.7). As freight increases and idle capacity is utilized, a reduction in average costs shows up immediately. Conversely, a downturn in volume, caused by a decline in activity, immediately blows out average costs because transport fleets must operate below capacity or stand idle.

Capital Goods

Capital goods spending is heavily influenced by actual orders as well as by changes in the level of capacity utilization (Exhibit 6.8). Rising rates of capacity utilization trigger investment in capital equipment while falling levels of capacity utilization result in a pronounced slowdown in business investment. The exchange rate is also significant in the performance of the capital goods sector (capital goods' exports are a major portion of the demand for U.S. capital goods).[4] Capital goods producers perform best when the economy is emerging from a period of depressed growth.

---

[4] In 1996, exports of capital goods (excluding autos) amounted to $252.6 billion and accounted for 41.3 percent of U.S. goods.

Exhibit 6.6 GDP-Sensitive Sectors' Relative Performance under Different Economic Conditions.

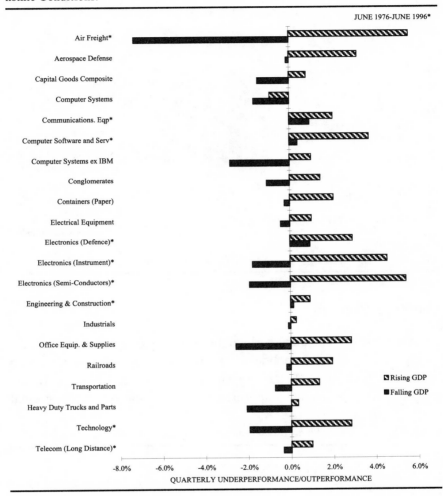

JUNE 1976-JUNE 1996*

QUARTERLY UNDERPERFORMANCE/OUTPERFORMANCE

* See Appendix 6.2.

Exhibit 6.7   GDP-Sensitive Sectors and GDP Growth.

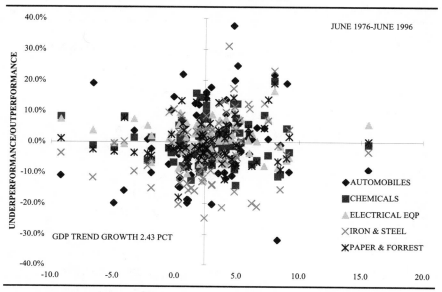

Consumer Cyclicals

From the mid-sixties to the early eighties, the auto sector experienced a long period of secular decline. It lost to both Japanese and European producers, and generally underperformed the overall market. In the early eighties, the industry appeared to recover and resumed a normal

Exhibit 6.8   Business Fixed Investment and the Capacity Utilization Rate.

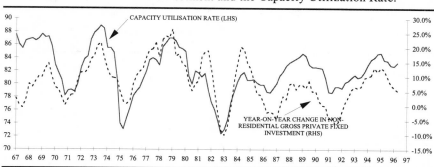

Data Source: Bureau of Economic Analysis and the Federal Reserve Board.

Exhibit 6.9 Consumer Cyclicals Relative Performance under Different Economic Conditions.

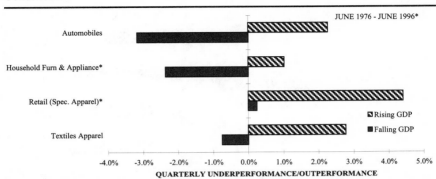

* See Appendix 6.2.

sector rotation pattern. The auto sector is extremely sensitive to changes in the economy and to disposable income (Exhibit 6.9). In large part, this is because of the leads and lags involved in production and the inventory control problem that constantly looms large for the industry.

Other consumer cyclical sectors, such as household furnishings and appliances, are sensitive to the economy in general and to interest rates given their impact on residential construction and new home purchases.

Textile and apparel stocks tend to rise and fall with the economy and consumer sentiment.

GROWTH AND INTEREST-SENSITIVE SECTORS

Construction and Housing

Residential construction is sensitive to both economic growth and the interest rate environment. The growth environment, does, however, appear to exert the dominant influence as is evident in Exhibit 6.10. Rising GDP results in outperformance of the housing sectors relative to the rest of the market, and falling GDP results in underperformance even though falling GDP is often associated with falling interest rates which are supportive of this sector.

Exhibit 6.10   Growth and Interest Sensitive Sectors' Relative Performance under Different Economic Conditions.

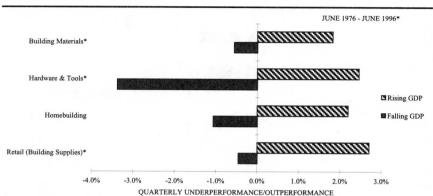

* See Appendix 6.2.

Housing is sensitive to the interest rate environment because of the importance of financing costs (Exhibit 6.11). Given the substantial impact of mortgage rates on the affordability of housing, changes in the level of 30-year mortgage interest rates have a major impact on housing demand and consequently on the profitability of housing activity. Additionally, the cost of capital for construction companies is quite significant as they use debt to fund construction in progress and unsold inventory.

Exhibit 6.11   GDP Growth and 10-Year U.S. Treasury Bond Yields.

INTEREST-SENSITIVE SECTORS

Several different industry categories are particularly sensitive to the interest rate environment—these sectors are banks, thrifts, financial service companies, insurance companies and utilities (Exhibit 6.12).

Banks and Financial Stocks

Banks and thrifts are sensitive to both the level of interest rates and the shape of the yield curve, or the spread between short- and long-term rates. Loan and credit demand is obviously influenced by the level of interest rates. Consequently, banks and thrifts tend to perform well in declining interest rate environments. Also, as net creditors, banks and thrifts suffer during periods of inflation (rising long-term interest rates) and benefit during periods of deflation (falling long-term interest rates).

The relative and absolute price performance of bank stocks is highly sensitive to changes in both long- and short-term interest rates. Over the 20-year period from September 1976 to June 1996, bank stock performance relative to the S&P 500 appears to have been heavily influenced

Exhibit 6.12 Interest Sensitive Sectors' Relative Performance under Different Economic Conditions.

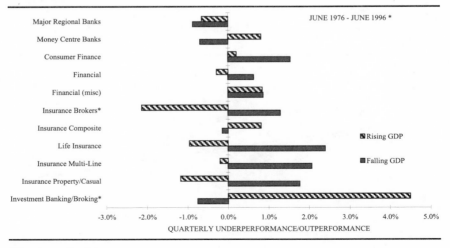

* See Appendix 6.2.

by changes in long-term interest rates, as illustrated in Exhibit 6.13. Sixty-six percent of the time, bank stocks' performance relative to the S&P 500 was correlated with the direction of interest rates. During periods of long-term rate declines, bank stocks outperformed the S&P 500 in 64 percent of the quarters. During quarters when interest rates were increasing, bank stocks underperformed the S&P 500 68 percent of the time.

Banks and thrifts are creditors with long-duration assets that are, by and large, funded by short-duration liabilities. These creditors are sensitive to changes in the absolute level of interest rates as well as the relationship between short- and long-term interest rates. Financial institutions generally benefit from declining interest rates and a steepening yield curve where the spread widens between lending and funding rates. Often, however, their sensitivity to rate changes and twists in the yield curve is somewhat less than anticipated given extensive interest rate gap management. In addition, the dismantling of credit controls and the deregulation of deposit rates in the late seventies and early eighties has eroded the impact that changes in the yield curve might have on bank performance. This is evident from Exhibit 6.14, which shows little correlation between bank stock price performance and changes in the slope of the yield curve.

Exhibit 6.13   Bank Stock Price Performance Relative to the S&P 500 and Interest Rate Changes.

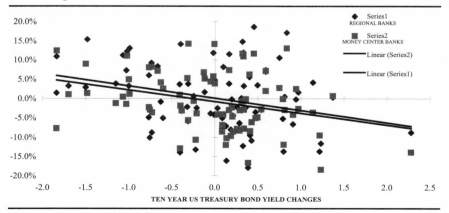

Exhibit 6.14   Relative Performance of Bank Stocks and Changes in the Yield Curve Spread.

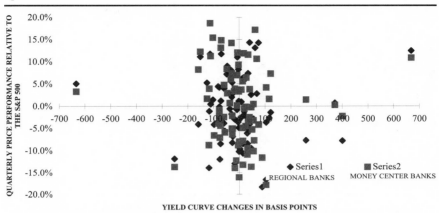

The high-inflation, high-interest-rate environment of the seventies and eighties detracted considerably from the relative performance of bank stocks, which underperformed the broader market for prolonged periods during the two decades. The recession of 1990–1991 brought a turning point for bank stocks. Inflation was finally wrung from the system, and bank stocks began a sustained period of outperformance.

Banks are also sensitive to customer debt repayment capacity, credit quality and loan delinquencies and write-offs. Any downturn in the economy tends to exacerbate these problem areas and detract from performance.

Insurance Companies

Like banks, insurance companies—both life and property/casualty insurers—are highly sensitive to the growth and interest rate environment. Insurance companies, on average, have outperformed the market during periods of declining growth and have underperformed during periods of accelerating growth. In large measure, this is due to the correlation of interest rates with GDP growth. Interest rate increases, all else being equal, are negative for insurance companies, and falling interest rates are positive for the price performance of insurance companies. The

Exhibit 6.15   Insurance Company Price Performance and Changes in Interest Rates.

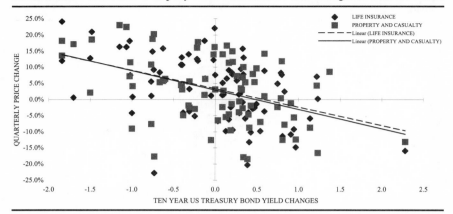

scatter diagram in Exhibit 6.15 shows the relationship between changes in 10-year U.S. Treasury bond yields and insurance company price changes. An important causal factor in this relationship is that insurance companies tend to have long-duration assets such as stocks, bonds and real estate, which are all sensitive to changes in interest rates.

Investment Banking and Brokering

Investment banks and brokering firms significantly outperform the market during periods of growth while underperforming, on average, during periods of declining growth. Robust economic performance underpins financial markets and corporate activity, providing a lucrative environment for these firms. The direction of interest rates, although important, is secondary to the overall performance of the economy and is exhibited most in the relative performance of financial assets.

STABLE GROWTH/DEFENSIVE STOCKS

Stable or defensive stocks are stocks that tend to have a low sensitivity to changes in the overall economy. These stocks tend to underperform during periods of strong economic growth and to outperform during economic downturns. In general, these companies possess limited pricing power and incur margin erosion during inflationary periods, but they fare relatively well when inflation is low. This is because of the considerable resistance of consumers to price increases.

Healthcare, Drugs and Cosmetics

Healthcare, drugs and cosmetics stocks are classic defensive stocks in that they tend to outperform in a declining market. Healthcare stocks performed exceptionally well in both rising and falling macroeconomic environments as Exhibit 6.16 indicates. In fact, both hospital management and managed healthcare companies have outperformed the market, on average, in all economic environments. This is largely caused by an increasing proportion of GDP being devoted to healthcare in the United States.

Defensive Consumer Sectors

Defensive consumer sectors are comprised of stocks that have had steady performance with minimal swings in response to changes in the economy. Food, beverages, alcohol, tobacco and the companies that distribute these goods tend to outperform the market during downturns because consumer expenditures on these categories are income-inelastic. These stocks tend to underperform during periods of economic growth given their lack of sensitivity to improving economic conditions.

These stocks are generally held during periods of economic decline given their relatively stable sales performance and improving input

Exhibit 6.16   Healthcare, Drug and Cosmetics Sectors' Relative Performance under Different Economic Conditions.

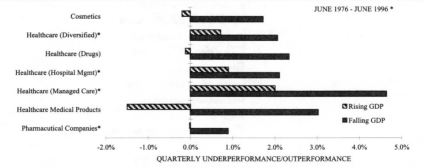

* See Appendix 6.2.

prices during downturns. Defensive consumer stocks often outperform
the market 3 to 6 months prior to a downturn, provided that recent economic growth has been above "sustainable" levels or a prolonged period
of strong to moderate growth has recently been experienced. In short,
when concerns about the economy emerge, investors move to these defensive sectors.

Utilities

As regulated entities, utilities encounter serious resistance to rate increases and, consequently, underperform in growth and inflationary environments. That is, utilities find it difficult to pass on input cost
increases because of regulatory constraints and the inherent time delays
in price changes. Utilities therefore tend to underperform the broad market during periods of economic growth. Their regulated pricing structure, however, provides considerable support when the economy turns
down as there is no pressure on prices or margins. In addition, their high
dividend payout policy tends to make them attractive during periods of
market weakness. With their high and stable dividend payouts, utilities

Exhibit 6.17   Defensive Consumer Sectors' Relative Performance under Different
Economic Conditions.

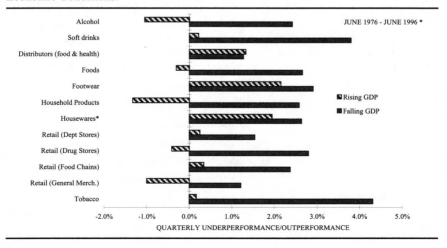

* See Appendix 6.2.

Exhibit 6.18 Utility Companies' Relative Peformance.

| | Rising GDP | Falling GDP |

JUNE 1976 - JUNE 1996 — QUARTERLY UNDERPERFORMANCE/OUTPERFORMANCE

-4.0% -3.0% -2.0% -1.0% 0.0% 1.0% 2.0%

Waste Management
Utilities
Telephone
Electric Companies

are often quite sensitive to interest rate changes. In some respects, they are viewed as a substitute for bonds.

Waste management companies have performed somewhat like growth stocks that outperform the market during periods of growth *and* decline. This is a result of the increasing privatization in this industry and the very strong growth experienced by these companies.

GROWTH STOCKS

Growth stocks are stocks that exhibit secular growth in earnings that are superior to the trend growth rate of the economy in general.[5] Growth stocks are characterized by high profit retention and profitability rates, low yields and high price-to-earnings ratios.[6]

---

[5] Some academics and analysts make a distinction between "growth stocks" and "growth companies." [See, for example, Frank K. Reilly, *Investment Analysis and Portfolio Management* (Harcourt Brace College Publishers, 1994), pp. 662–663.] The distinction is as follows: a growth company is a company that can make investments that yield returns above the firm's required rate of return. [Ezra Solomon, *The Theory of Financial Management* (New York: Columbia University Press, 1963), pp. 55–68; and Merton Miller and Franco Modigliani, "Dividend Policy, Growth and the Valuation of Shares," *Journal of Business, 34,* no. 4 (October 1961), pp. 411–433.] In contrast, growth stocks are stocks that yield a higher rate of return than other stocks with similar risk.

[6] A number of papers have focused on the usefulness of a single measure (the price–book ratio) for screening growth companies. The rationale is that the price represents an assessment of future prospects and the book value represents past costs. The greater the future prospects, the greater the future prospects to embedded costs. See, for example, Barr Rosenberg, Kenneth Reid, and Ronald Lanstein, "Persuasive Evidence of Market Inefficiency," *Journal of Portfolio Management* (Spring 1985); and Carlo Capaul, Ian Rowley, and William F. Sharpe, "International Value and Growth Stock Returns," *Financial Analysts Journal* (February, 1993), pp. 27–36.

Exhibit 6.19 Sector and Industry Rotation and the Business Cycle.

| | | Business Cycle Phase and Relative Performance | |
Major Industries	Dominant Investment Characteristic	Outperformance	Underperformance
	Basic and Industrial Materials		
Aluminum, chemicals, mining, iron and steel, machinery, paper and forest products.	Intermediate producers, high fixed costs, benefit immediately from volume increases, capacity fixed in the short run with long lead times necessary for capacity increases. Benefit form capacity constraints late in the cycle when capacity utilization rates are high.	Outperforms following mid-cycle pause or recession, often anticipating resumption of growth by one or two quarters. Periods of high-capacity utilization and positive output gap. Strong outperformance during strong growth periods.	Underperforms during periods of moderating growth and increasing output gaps.
	Energy and Oil		
Natural gas, oil and gas drilling and equipment, integrated oil, oil exploration and international oil.	Driven by global energy prices, which are heavily influenced by the OPEC cartel.	Outperforms when oil prices increase significantly. Outperformance contemporaneous with oil price changes.	Underperforms when oil prices decline.
	GDP Growth-Sensitive Industrial Sector		
Air freight, aerospace, capital goods, computer systems and software, communications equipment, conglomerates, containers, electrical equipment, electronics, engineering and construction, railroads, transportation, technology and telecommunications.	Industrial sectors most sensitive to changes in GDP. Capital goods influenced by industrial capacity utilization rate and investment spending cycle, which tends to lag the economic cycle. Also influenced by the exchange rate, given high export component. Transportation sensitive to increases in freight shipments.	Outperforms early in an upturn, occasionally leading recovery by one or two quarters. best performance during periods of sharp recovery following weak growth period.	Underperforms during early recessions and mid-cycle pauses, often anticipating downturn by one quarter.

Industries	Characteristics	Outperforms	Underperforms
Automobiles, household furnishings and appliances, specialty retail and textiles.	Profits tend to be driven by the business cycle.	Outperforms early in the cyclical upturn and during the mid-cycle when growth is above trend.	Underperforms during early downturns and late and mid-cycle pauses.

GDP Growth and Interest Sensitive Sector

Construction, housing and building-related.	Sensitive to both interest rates and GDP growth.	Strong recovery following initial downturn. Outperforms early in the cycle, often anticipating recovery.	Underperforms late in the cycle when interest rates are rising and the economy is turning down.

Interest-Sensitive Sector

Banks, thrifts, life and casualty insurance, investment banking and brokering.	Acutely sensitive to interest rates. Investment banks and brokering very sensitive to GDP performance.	Outperforms second half of recessions and mid-cycle slowdowns as monetary policy eases. Performs well during periods of moderate to weak growth.	Underperforms during periods of excessive growth, when interest rate pressures are evident. Lag during late cycle and in early part of recessions, when rates are increasing.

Defensive Consumer Sector

Alcohol, soft drinks, foods, household products, retail drug stores, retail food stores and tobacco.	Staple consumer products; "necessities" with little consumption variability and hence little profit variability.	Outperforms during *sharp* economic downturns. Often outperforms three to six months before a GDP correction following periods of "nonsustainable growth" or extended periods of moderate growth.	Lag in early bull markets when an upturn in economic activity is anticipated.

(Continued)

Exhibit 6.19 *(Continued)*

Major Industries	Dominant Investment Characteristic	Business Cycle Phase and Relative Performance	
		Outperformance	Underperformance
	Health Care and Cosmetic		
Cosmetics, drugs, hospital management, managed care, medical products and pharmaceuticals.	Growth companies enjoying long-term secular outperformance as percent of GDP devoted to healthcare increases. Subject to regulatory uncertainty and volatility.	Outperforms in downturns.	Underperforms during strong upturns.
	Entertainment and Leisure		
Entertainment, leisure products, hotels, restaurants, publishing.	Sensitive to consumer sentiment and disposable income.	Outperforms in early growth phase.	Underperforms in early recessions and major downturns.
	Utilities		
Utilities, telephone, electric, waste management.	Regulated pricing.	Outperforms during bear markets, when growth is flagging.	Underperforms in strong markets.

Growth companies tend to be concentrated in areas where major secular trends are presenting above-normal investment and growth opportunities. Familiar examples are technology-based companies, drug and biotech companies and companies benefiting from social issues such as pollution control and increased concern about health care. These sectors may outperform the market for significant periods of time, but they can also be extremely volatile. Growth stocks often lag during the initial stage of a bull market, and they take on defensive characteristics in bear markets.

Because growth companies tend to reinvest earnings rather than pay them out in the form of dividends, growth stocks are acutely sensitive to changes in interest rates. Rate changes result in changes in the discount rate applied to the future stream of expected income. That is, because current income is deferred in favor of reinvestment in the business, which is assumed to generate a return higher than that available in the investment arena in general, any changes in the discount factor applied to the deferred income stream has a major impact on the present value of expected future income.

SELECTED REFERENCES

Capaul, Carlo, Rowley, Ian, and Sharpe, William F. "International Value and Growth Stock Returns," *Financial Analysts Journal* (February, 1993), pp. 27–36.

Farrell, James L. *Guide to Portfolio Management.* New York: McGraw-Hill, 1983.

Farrell, James L. "Homogeneous Stock Groupings: Implications for Portfolio Management," *Financial Analysts Journal* (May–June 1975), pp. 50–62.

Rosenberg, Barr, Reid, Kenneth, and Lanstein, Ronald. "Persuasive Evidence of Market Inefficiency," *Journal of Portfolio Management* (Spring 1985).

Appendix 6.1   Standard & Poor's 500 Stock Market Index.

Industry Group	Market Weight %	Number of Stocks
GDP Growth Sensitive		
Aerospace		
Aerospace/Defense	2.111	8
Air Freight		
Airlines		
Airlines	0.345	4
Autos		
Automobiles	1.978	3
Autoparts After Mkt.	0.317	4
Capital Goods		
Manufactured— Diversified	0.996	10
Machinery— Diversified	0.865	10
Pollution Control	0.488	3
Machines	0.025	2
Chemicals		
Chemicals	2.406	10
Chemicals— Diversified	0.349	4
Chemicals—Special	0.412	5
Electrical Equipment		
Electrical Cos.	3.132	26
Electrical Equipment	3.848	9
Electronics		
Electronic Defense	0.018	1
Electronic Instruments	0.070	2
Electronic Semiconductors	2.453	8
Information Processing		
Computer Systems	3.206	14
Computer Software	3.189	10
Energy		
Oil & Gas Drilling	0.048	2
Oil—Integ. Domestic	1.395	11
Oil—Integ. International	6.631	6
Oil—Well Eqpmt. & Svcs.	0.830	6
Oil—Explor. & Production	0.171	3
Natural Gas	0.948	14

Appendix 6.1 *(Continued)*

Industry Group	Market Weight %	Number of Stocks
Homebuilding		
Building Materials	0.208	3
Household Furn. &Appl.	0.161	3
Hardware & Tools	0.156	3
Homebuilding	0.040	3
Manufactured Housing	0.019	1
Multi-Industry Conglomerates		
Conglomerates	0.319	2
Paper & Containers		
Containers Paper	0.114	3
Paper & Forest Prod.	1.044	12
Railroads & Trucking		
Engineering & Construction	0.142	2
Heavy Trucks & Parts	0.282	6
Truckers	0.041	3
Railroads	1.076	5
Transportation—Misc.	0.130	2
Steel & Nonferrous Metals		
Aluminum	0.435	3
Containers, Metal & Glass	0.135	2
Gold	0.573	7
Metals—Misc.	0.368	5
Steel	0.295	7
Interest Rate Sensitive		
Banks & Thrifts		
Major Regional Banks	4.754	22
Money Center Banks	2.783	6
Personal Loans	0.214	2
Savings & Loans	0.193	3
Financial Services		
Financial—Misc.	1.924	7
Invest Bnk/Brkrge Firms	1.048	5
Insurance		
Insurance Brokers	0.258	3
Life Insurance	0.616	7
Multiline Insurance	1.203	3
Property/Casualty Ins.	1.257	8

(Continued)

Appendix 6.1   *(Continued)*

Industry Group	Market Weight %	Number of Stocks
Stable Growth/Defensive		
Communications		
Communication—Equip.	1.607	10
Telecomm—Long Dist	2.562	4
Telephone	4.158	9
Drugs & Cosmetics		
Cosmetics	0.822	4
Drugs	4.031	5
Lodging & Gaming		
Hotel/Motel	0.410	4
Healthcare Services		
Health Care	4.111	7
Health Care HMOs	0.203	2
Health Care—Misc.	0.418	4
Hospital Mgmt.	0.621	3
Medical Products	0.978	9
Food & Beverages/Tobacco		
Beverages—Alcoholic	0.696	4
Beverages—Soft Drink	3.454	2
Foods	2.913	13
Tobacco	1.755	3
Entertainment		
Entertainment	1.296	4
Leisure Time	0.076	3
Restaurants	0.758	6
Publishing/Broadcasting		
Broadcasting Media	0.437	3
Photography/Imaging	0.542	2
Publishing	0.304	3
Publishing—Newspaper	0.575	6
Specialty Printing	0.178	3
Retail		
Distributors Index	0.169	3
Household Products	2.010	4
Housewares	0.235	10
Retail Stores—Apparel	0.362	4
Retail Stores—Dept.	0.797	6
Retail Stores—Drugs	0.234	3

Appendix 6.1 *(Continued)*

Industry Group	Market Weight %	Number of Stocks
Stable Growth/Defensive		
Retail (continued)		
Retail Stores—Food	0.609	6
Retail Stores—Gen.	1.810	4
Retail Stores—Spec.	1.181	9
Shoes	0.360	3
Textiles Industry	0.212	5
Toys	0.211	2
Others		
Miscellaneous	1.455	10
Specialized Services	0.660	8
Office Eqpmt. & Supp.	0.657	4

*Capitalization-weighted index of 500 stocks as of September 4, 1996.

Data Source: Bloomberg.

Appendix 6.2   Industry and Sector Price Performance Relative to the S&P 500 under Different Economic Conditions.

	(Quarterly Observations, June 1976–June 1996)*					
	Growth above Trend & Rising	Growth above Trend & Falling	Growth below Trend & Rising	Growth below Trend & Falling	Growth Rising	Growth Falling
Aerospace Defense						
Outperformance/Underperformance	3.00%	1.14%	3.59%	−1.01%	3.20%	−0.13%
Standard Deviation	8.40%	8.66%	6.57%	6.57%	7.76%	7.62%
No. of Observations	28	16	14	23	42	39
Air Freight						
Outperformance/Underperformance	9.05%	−6.86%	−0.10%	−7.56%	5.62%	−7.27%
Standard Deviation	14.23%	5.52%	12.18%	8.63%	13.85%	7.31%
No. of Observations (6/88–6/96)	10	7	6	10	16	17
Aluminum						
Outperformance/Underperformance	0.86%	2.52%	−0.67%	−2.74%	0.35%	−0.58%
Standard Deviation	9.76%	10.95%	12.29%	14.04%	10.54%	12.97%
No. of Observations	28	16	14	23	42	39
Auto Parts after Market						
Outperformance/Underperformance	−1.90%	−0.24%	2.50%	−0.12%	−0.43%	−0.17%
Standard Deviation	8.12%	6.58%	6.79%	7.72%	7.90%	7.18%
No. of Observations	28	16	14	23	42	39
Automobiles						
Outperformance/Underperformance	1.03%	1.19%	4.73%	−6.21%	2.27%	−3.17%
Standard Deviation	14.09%	9.63%	7.90%	10.87%	12.39%	10.89%
No. of Observations	28	16	14	23	42	39
Banks, Composite						
Outperformance/Underperformance	0.09%	0.73%	4.97%	−1.94%	2.04%	−0.84%
Standard Deviation	8.90%	6.18%	4.36%	9.18%	7.63%	7.97%
No. of Observations (9/80–6/96)	9	7	6	10	15	17
Banks, Major Regional						
Outperformance/Underperformance	−0.69%	−0.02%	−0.55%	−1.45%	−0.64%	−0.86
Standard Deviation	6.99%	7.69%	7.78%	7.88%	7.17%	7.73%
No. of Observations	28	16	14	23	42	39
Banks, Money Center						
Outperformance/Underperformance	0.44%	−0.20%	1.58%	−1.02%	0.82%	−0.69%
Standard Deviation	8.65%	6.99%	9.00%	9.25%	8.67%	8.31%
No. of Observations	28	16	14	23	42	39
Beverages (Alcoholic)						
Outperformance/Underperformance	−1.40%	4.05%	−0.34%	1.28%	−1.05%	2.42%
Standard Deviation	7.62%	7.81%	6.62%	8.71%	7.24%	8.36%
No. of Observations	28	16	14	23	42	39
Beverages (Soft Drinks)						
Outperformance/Underperformance	1.08%	4.42%	−1.49%	3.38%	0.22%	3.80%
Standard Deviation	6.39%	7.26%	7.21%	6.46%	6.70%	6.73%
No. of Observations	28	16	14	23	42	39

Appendix 6.2   *(Continued)*

(Quarterly Observations, June 1976–June 1996)*						
	Growth above Trend & Rising	Growth above Trend & Falling	Growth below Trend & Rising	Growth below Trend & Falling	Growth Rising	Growth Falling
Broadcast Media						
Outperformance/Underperformance	2.87%	4.79%	1.43%	−0.05%	2.39%	1.94%
Standard Deviation	9.14%	9.07%	7.57%	7.05%	8.58%	8.19%
No. of Observations	28	16	14	23	42	39
Building Materials						
Outperformance/Underperformance	1.39%	−2.57%	2.80%	1.16%	1.82%	−0.56%
Standard Deviation	9.60%	6.08%	10.54%	13.76%	9.83%	10.88%
No. of Observations (12/82–6/96)	20	12	9	14	29	26
Capital Goods, Composite						
Outperformance/Underperformance	0.93%	−0.65%	0.52%	−2.05%	0.80%	−1.47%
Standard Deviation	4.14%	3.74%	4.49%	3.23%	4.21%	3.47%
No. of Observations	28	16	14	23	42	39
Chemicals						
Outperformance/Underperformance	0.30%	−0.13%	−0.62%	−1.11%	−0.01%	−0.70%
Standard Deviation	6.83%	7.57%	7.71%	5.76%	7.05%	6.49%
No. of Observations	28	16	14	23	42	39
Chemicals, Composite						
Outperformance/Underperformance	0.72%	1.03%	3.55%	−3.20%	2.02%	−1.79%
Standard Deviation	7.01%	5.65%	7.24%	4.77%	6.97%	5.25%
No. of Observations (6/90–6/96)	7	4	6	8	13	12
Chemicals, Diversified						
Outperformance/Underperformance	2.30%	0.96%	0.84%	−2.15%	1.79%	−0.93%
Standard Deviation	5.77%	5.14%	6.45%	4.57%	5.97%	4.97%
No. of Observations (12/79–6/96)	22	13	12	20	34	33
Chemicals, Specialty						
Outperformance/Underperformance	0.19%	−0.57%	−0.02%	0.25%	0.12%	−0.11%
Standard Deviation	9.09%	4.45%	4.25%	4.89%	7.71%	4.62%
No. of Observations (6/84–6/96)	16	11	8	14	24	25
Comm. Equipment						
Outperformance/Underperformance	1.68%	2.53%	2.85%	−0.08%	2.05%	0.96%
Standard Deviation	15.10%	12.90%	14.11%	7.14%	14.56%	9.73%
No. of Observations (6/81–6/96)	21	12	10	18	31	30
Composite						
Outperformance/Underperformance	2.18%	1.67%	0.64%	2.60%	1.73%	2.22%
Standard Deviation	8.41%	4.71%	8.62%	8.44%	8.43%	7.13%
No. of Observations	47	24	19	35	66	59
Computer Software & Service						
Outperformance/Underperformance	2.76%	1.80%	5.78%	−0.61%	3.73%	0.39%
Standard Deviation	7.53%	9.84%	5.27%	9.13%	6.94%	9.33%
No. of Observations (9/81–6/96)	21	12	10	17	31	29

(Continued)

Appendix 6.2   *(Continued)*

	Growth above Trend & Rising	Growth above Trend & Falling	Growth below Trend & Rising	Growth below Trend & Falling	Growth Rising	Growth Falling
(Quarterly Observations, June 1976–June 1996)*						
Computer Systems						
Outperformance/Underperformance	−0.08%	0.19%	−2.55%	−2.94%	−0.90%	−1.66%
Standard Deviation	10.20%	7.96%	9.00%	7.58%	9.78%	7.79%
No. of observations	28	16	14	23	42	39
Computer Systems EXCL IBM						
Outperformance/Underperformance	1.46%	−0.22%	0.12%	−4.56%	1.02%	−2.78%
Standard Deviation	10.39%	11.45%	10.66%	7.75%	10.37%	9.55%
No. of Observations	28	16	14	23	42	39
Conglomerates						
Outperformance/Underperformance	1.02%	−0.38%	2.32%	−1.53%	1.45%	−1.06%
Standard Deviation	5.59%	5.60%	7.04%	5.50%	6.05%	5.50%
No. of Observations	28	16	14	23	42	39
Consumer Finance						
Outperformance/Underperformance	−1.92%	3.21%	4.48%	0.46%	0.21%	1.54%
Standard Deviation	7.88%	6.36%	15.79%	12.12%	11.37%	10.22%
No. of Observations	28	15	14	23	42	39
Containers, Metal & Glass						
Outperformance/Underperformance	0.92%	1.94%	1.07%	0.37%	0.97%	1.02%
Standard Deviation	8.20%	7.65%	7.88%	5.50%	8.00%	6.42%
No. of Observations	28	16	14	23	42	39
Containers, Paper						
Outperformance/Underperformance	2.81%	0.31%	0.56%	−0.63%	2.06%	−0.24%
Standard Deviation	10.30%	9.43%	10.71%	8.70%	10.36%	8.90%
No. of Observations	28	16	14	23	42	39
Cosmetics						
Outperformance/Underperformance	0.44%	1.21%	−1.46%	2.09%	−0.19%	1.73%
Standard Deviation	6.65%	6.95%	5.72%	8.30%	6.35%	7.69%
No. of Observations	28	16	14	23	42	39
Electrical Equipment						
Outperformance/Underperformance	0.54%	0.86%	1.99%	−1.30%	1.02%	−0.42%
Standard Deviation	4.79%	6.26%	4.13%	5.63%	4.58%	5.92%
No. of Observations	28	16	14	23	42	39
Electronics, Defense						
Outperformance/Underperformance	−0.21%	0.98%	8.43%	0.93%	2.93%	0.95%
Standard Deviation	6.37%	6.44%	14.51%	8.38%	10.65%	7.48%
No. of Observations (3/86–6/96)	14	8	8	12	22	20
Electronics, Instrument						
Outperformance/Underperformance	3.84%	−0.88%	5.94%	−2.36%	4.56%	−1.76%
Standard Deviation	13.85%	8.20%	13.89%	7.79%	13.73%	7.88%
No. of Observations (3/77–6/96)	27	15	14	22	41	37

Appendix 6.2 *(Continued)*

(Quarterly Observations, June 1976–June 1996)*						
	Growth above Trend & Rising	Growth above Trend & Falling	Growth below Trend & Rising	Growth below Trend & Falling	Growth Rising	Growth Falling
Electronics, Semiconductors						
Outperformance/Underperformance	3.93%	0.68%	8.31%	−3.67%	5.43%	−1.91%
Standard Deviation	13.77%	11.41%	12.36%	11.10%	13.32%	11.28%
No. of Observations	27	15	14	22	41	37
Energy, Composite						
Outperformance/Underperformance	−2.56%	0.44%	−2.33%	1.44%	−2.47%	1.03%
Standard Deviation	5.35%	4.60%	4.43%	9.15%	4.84%	7.44%
No. of Observations (9/80–6/96)	9	7	6	10	15	17
Engineering & Construction						
Outperformance/Underperformance	1.01%	1.57%	0.82%	−0.70%	0.93%	0.15%
Standard Deviation	9.40%	16.34%	8.10%	8.36%	8.60%	11.50%
No. of Observations (3/88–6/96)	9	6	6	10	15	16
Entertainment						
Outperformance/Underperformance	5.04%	1.95%	−3.40%	1.27%	2.23%	1.54%
Standard Deviation	9.67%	9.23%	6.51%	9.16%	9.55%	9.07%
No. of Observations (9/76–6/96)	28	15	14	23	42	38
Entertainment & Leisure, Composite						
Outperformance/Underperformance	3.66%	−0.48%	0.96%	−1.36%	2.41%	−1.07%
Standard Deviation	11.18%	6.25%	6.39%	5.25%	9.03%	5.33%
No. of Observations (6/90–6/96)	7	4	6	8	13	12
Financial						
Outperformance/Underperformance	−0.62%	0.66%	0.41%	0.63%	−0.28%	0.64%
Standard Deviation	5.59%	6.02%	6.45%	6.37%	5.83%	6.15%
No. of Observations (9/76–6/96)	28	15	14	23	42	38
Foods						
Outperformance/Underperformance	0.63%	3.34%	−2.20%	2.18%	−0.31%	2.66%
Standard Deviation	5.61%	6.18%	4.30%	6.20%	5.33%	6.14%
No. of Observations	28	16	14	23	42	39
Footwear						
Outperformance/Underperformance	3.39%	1.30%	−0.32%	4.03%	2.15%	2.91%
Standard Deviation	11.30%	12.35%	12.46%	11.92%	11.68%	12.02%
No. of Observations	28	16	14	23	42	39
Goldmining						
Outperformance/Underperformance	−0.31%	0.60%	10.06%	−1.19%	3.14%	−0.46%
Standard Deviation	14.53%	19.77%	23.82%	20.99%	18.53%	20.25%
No. of Observations	28	16	14	23	42	39
Hardware & Tools						
Outperformance/Underperformance	3.67%	−3.35%	−0.25%	−3.41%	2.46%	−3.38%
Standard Deviation	8.95%	5.96%	5.04%	6.26%	8.06%	6.00%
No. of Observations (9/83–6/96)	18	12	8	14	26	26

(Continued)

Appendix 6.2   *(Continued)*

	Growth above Trend & Rising	Growth above Trend & Falling	Growth below Trend & Rising	Growth below Trend & Falling	Growth Rising	Growth Falling
(Quarterly Observations, June 1976–June 1996)*						
Healthcare, Composite						
Outperformance/Underperformance	0.01%	0.44%	−0.33%	2.48%	−0.10%	1.62%
Standard Deviation	4.69%	6.55%	4.24%	7.75%	4.42%	7.15%
No. of Observations (6/87–6/96)	12	8	6	11	18	19
Healthcare, Diversified						
Outperformance/Underperformance	1.44%	−0.02%	−0.54%	3.37%	0.72%	2.07%
Standard Deviation	5.56%	8.01%	3.05%	7.76%	4.81%	7.84%
No. of Observations (12/85–6/96)	14	8	8	13	22	21
Healthcare, Drugs						
Outperformance/Underperformance	0.25%	0.51%	−0.83%	3.62%	−0.11%	2.34%
Standard Deviation	5.80%	7.03%	6.01%	6.37%	5.82%	6.73%
No. of Observations	28	16	14	23	42	39
Healthcare, Hospital Management						
Outperformance/Underperformance	−1.24%	1.24%	4.72%	2.68%	0.91%	2.11%
Standard Deviation	8.51%	11.66%	12.36%	18.71%	10.31%	16.10%
No. of Observations (9/79–6/96)	23	13	13	20	36	33
Healthcare, Managed Care						
Outperformance/Underperformance	5.78%	6.32%	−3.65%	2.43%	2.01%	4.65%
Standard Deviation	12.70%	13.03%	15.51%	19.57%	13.91%	14.73%
No. of Observations (6/92–6/96)	6	4	4	3	10	7
Health Care, Medical Products						
Outperformance/Underperformance	−1.76%	0.02%	−0.94%	5.13%	−1.49%	3.03%
Standard Deviation	7.73%	4.57%	7.26%	7.60%	7.50%	6.94%
No. of Observations	28	16	14	23	42	39
Healthcare, Miscellaneous						
Outperformance/Underperformance	−2.06%	−3.61%	−1.29%	1.98%	−1.80%	−0.37%
Standard Deviation	17.32%	15.04%	8.68%	16.60%	14.71%	15.78%
No. of Observations (6/87–6/96)	12	8	6	11	18	19
Homebuilding						
Outperformance/Underperformance	0.61%	−3.23%	5.13%	0.28%	2.20%	−1.06%
Standard Deviation	15.35%	16.35%	14.41%	16.00%	14.99%	15.98%
No. of Observations (12/87–6/96)	24	13	13	21	37	34
Hotel/Motel						
Outperformance/Underperformance	0.57%	2.92%	8.13%	0.46%	3.09%	1.47%
Standard Deviation	12.78%	15.25%	14.47%	13.42%	13.67%	14.06%
No. of Observations	28	16	14	23	42	39
Household Furn. & Appliances						
Outperformance/Underperformance	0.62%	−3.08%	1.90%	−1.79%	1.02%	−2.36%
Standard Deviation	10.73%	5.98%	8.56%	8.10%	9.97%	7.13
No. of Observations (9/82–6/96)	20	12	9	15	29	27

Appendix 6.2 *(Continued)*

	Growth above Trend & Rising	Growth above Trend & Falling	Growth below Trend & Rising	Growth below Trend & Falling	Growth Rising	Growth Falling
(Quarterly Observations, June 1976–June 1996)*						
Household Products						
Outperformance/Underperformance	−0.17%	1.93%	−3.63%	3.03%	−1.33%	2.58%
Standard Deviation	7.38%	4.21%	5.53%	6.24%	6.95%	5.46%
No. of Observations	28	16	14	23	42	39
Housewares						
Outperformance/Underperformance	3.05%	0.23%	−0.29%	4.53%	1.94%	2.64%
Standard Deviation (6/84–6/96)	5.94%	10.27%	11.67%	9.95%	8.19%	10.11%
No. of Observations	16	11	8	14	24	25
Industrials						
Outperformance/Underperformance	0.29%	−0.05%	0.23%	−0.15%	0.27%	−0.11%
Standard Deviation	0.99%	0.81%	0.77%	0.64%	0.92%	0.70%
No. of Observations	39	19	19	32	58	51
Insurance, Brokers						
Outperformance/Underperformance	−1.05%	1.96%	−4.29%	0.76%	−2.13%	1.29%
Standard Deviation	7.22%	5.94%	9.78%	5.73%	8.10%	5.73%
No. of Observations (6/84–6/96)	16	11	8	14	24	25
Insurance, Composite						
Outperformance/Underperformance	1.44%	0.27%	0.10%	−0.34%	0.82%	−0.14%
Standard Deviation	6.78%	5.83%	5.88%	6.40%	6.16%	5.95%
No. of Observations (6/90–6/96)	7	4	6	8	13	12
Insurance, Life						
Outperformance/Underperformance	−1.97%	3.77%	1.09%	1.45%	−0.95%	2.40%
Standard Deviation	7.61%	7.75%	8.62%	6.82%	7.99%	7.21%
No. of Observations	28	16	14	23	42	39
Insurance, Multiline						
Outperformance/Underperformance	0.10%	1.56%	−0.82%	2.42%	−0.20%	2.07%
Standard Deviation	7.44%	7.19%	7.90%	8.13%	7.51%	7.67%
No. of Observations	28	16	14	23	42	39
Insurance, Property/Casualty						
Outperformance/Underperformance	−0.60%	0.17%	−2.31%	2.87%	−1.17%	1.77%
Standard Deviation	7.47%	7.00%	5.82%	7.73%	6.94%	7.47%
No. of Observations	28	16	14	23	42	39
Investment Banking/Brokering						
Outperformance/Underperformance	0.04%	−2.64%	11.18%	1.77%	4.50%	−0.75%
Standard Deviation	8.38%	3.35%	5.50%	9.60%	9.07	6.47%
No. of Observations (6/92–6/96)	6	4	4	3	10	7
Iron & Steel						
Outperformance/Underperformance	1.65%	−1.29%	−2.83%	−6.63%	0.15%	−4.44%
Standard Deviation	11.22%	11.88%	6.82%	9.72%	10.11%	10.84%
No. of Observations	28	16	14	23	42	39

(Continued)

Appendix 6.2   *(Continued)*

	Growth above Trend & Rising	Growth above Trend & Falling	Growth below Trend & Rising	Growth below Trend & Falling	Growth Rising	Growth Falling
(Quarterly Observations, June 1976–June 1996)*						
Leisure-Time Products						
Outperformance/Underperformance	−1.15%	2.76%	7.62%	1.18%	1.78%	1.83%
Standard Deviation	11.68%	12.28%	15.95%	11.28%	13.71%	11.57%
No. of Observations	28	16	14	23	42	39
Machinery, Diversified						
Outperformance/Underperformance	0.85%	−0.14%	2.83%	−1.86%	1.60%	−1.17%
Standard Deviation	7.85%	10.67%	8.09%	5.99%	7.80%	7.97%
No. of Observations (6/86–6/96)	13	8	8	12	21	20
Metals, Mining						
Outperformance/Underperformance	2.51%	2.01%	1.52%	−4.79%	2.18%	−2.00%
Standard Deviation	12.33%	13.27%	11.77%	11.29%	12.01%	12.44%
No. of Observations	28	16	14	23	42	39
Natural Gas						
Outperformance/Underperformance	1.18%	−0.56%	−1.88%	−0.16%	0.16%	−0.33%
Standard Deviation	9.22%	7.43%	7.44%	8.85%	8.70%	8.20%
No. of Observations	28	16	14	23	42	39
Office Eqpmt. & Supplies						
Outperformance/Underperformance	3.68%	−1.96%	1.34%	−2.98%	2.85%	−2.58%
Standard Deviation	5.23%	4.70%	11.91%	6.93%	7.92%	6.02%
No. of Observations (6/86–6/96)	11	7	6	11	17	18
Oil, Composite						
Outperformance/Underperformance	0.75%	−0.58%	0.60%	−0.18%	0.70%	−0.34%
Standard Deviation	6.40%	5.77%	7.42%	8.50%	6.67%	7.42%
No. of Observations	28	16	14	23	42	39
Oil, Dom. Integrated						
Outperformance/Underperformance	0.45%	−0.42%	0.73%	−1.44%	0.54%	−1.02%
Standard Deviation	8.77%	6.47%	8.80%	10.42%	8.68%	8.93%
No. of Observations	28	16	14	23	42	39
Oil, Expl. & Product						
Outperformance/Underperformance	0.63%	−4.75%	−8.38%	−1.46%	−3.23%	−2.56%
Standard Deviation	19.64%	7.00%	7.44%	21.30%	15.82%	17.56%
No. of Observations (6/89–6/96)	8	5	6	10	14	15
Oil & Gas Drilling & Eqpmt.						
Outperformance/Underperformance	0.24%	−1.99%	1.54%	−0.46%	0.67%	−1.09%
Standard Deviation	11.62%	9.12%	8.47%	11.80%	10.59%	10.68%
No. of Observations	28	16	14	23	42	39
Oil, Internatl. Integrated						
Outperformance/Underperformance	0.63%	−0.24%	0.18%	0.36%	0.48%	0.12%
Standard Deviation	5.80%	6.16%	7.70%	7.69%	6.40%	7.02%
No. of Observations	28	16	14	23	42	39

Appendix 6.2 *(Continued)*

	Growth above Trend & Rising	Growth above Trend & Falling	Growth below Trend & Rising	Growth below Trend & Falling	Growth Rising	Growth Falling
(Quarterly Observations, June 1976–June 1996)*						
Paper & Forest Products						
Outperformance/Underperformance	−0.32%	0.76%	0.55%	−2.38%	−0.03%	−1.09%
Standard Deviation	7.29%	7.40%	5.13%	5.79%	6.59%	6.59%
No. of Observations	28	16	14	23	42	39
Pharmaceuticals, Composite						
Outperformance/Underperformance	0.60%	−0.07%	−1.10%	1.67%	−0.02%	0.90%
Standard Deviation	6.68%	9.42%	4.23%	11.11%	5.73%	9.79%
No. of Observations (9/91–6/96)	7	4	4	5	11	9
Photo/Imaging						
Outperformance/Underperformance	−1.72%	−0.67%	−0.26%	4.52%	−1.05%	2.79%
Standard Deviation	9.51%	5.23%	8.73%	10.14%	8.81%	8.91%
No. of Observations (6/90–6/96)	7	4	6	8	13	12
Printing, Specialty						
Outperformance/Underperformance	−2.07%	0.06%	−5.38%	−2.57%	−3.40%	−1.25%
Standard Deviation	3.62%	5.39%	6.05%	10.05%	4.36%	6.75%
No. of Observations (6/94–6/96)	3	2	2	2	5	4
Publishing						
Outperformance/Underperformance	1.53%	1.56%	0.24%	1.51%	1.10%	1.53%
Standard Deviation	5.97%	5.16%	7.44%	8.77%	6.43%	7.42%
No. of Observations	28	16	14	23	42	39
Publishing, Newspapers						
Outperformance/Underperformance	1.24%	1.95%	1.10%	−0.64%	1.19%	0.42%
Standard Deviation	7.99%	7.52%	9.37%	8.52%	8.36%	8.13%
No. of Observations	28	16	14	23	42	39
Railroads						
Outperformance/Underperformance	1.63%	−0.40%	2.59%	−0.06%	1.95%	−0.20%
Standard Deviation	5.31%	5.06%	8.76%	6.47%	6.56%	5.88%
No. of Observations	28	15	14	23	42	39
Restaurants						
Outperformance/Underperformance	0.85%	2.40%	−0.45%	2.80%	0.42%	2.64%
Standard Deviation	7.44%	8.76%	6.61%	7.17%	7.12%	7.75%
No. of Observations	28	16	14	23	42	39
Retail, Building Supplies						
Outperformance/Underperformance	5.05%	−3.89%	−1.98%	1.77%	2.71%	−0.45%
Standard Deviation	9.56%	6.20%	7.22%	10.03%	9.32%	9.02%
No. of Observations (12/84–6/96)	16	9	8	14	24	23
Retail, Dept. Stores						
Outperformance/Underperformance	−0.84%	−0.29%	2.42%	2.81%	0.25%	1.54%
Standard Deviation	7.14%	9.88%	6.23%	12.15%	6.95%	11.24%
No. of Observations	28	16	14	23	42	39

(Continued)

Appendix 6.2   *(Continued)*

	Growth above Trend & Rising	Growth above Trend & Falling	Growth below Trend & Rising	Growth below Trend & Falling	Growth Rising	Growth Falling
\multicolumn{7}{c}{(Quarterly Observations, June 1976–June 1996)*}						
Retail, Drug Stores						
Outperformance/Underperformance	−0.69%	3.17%	0.15%	2.55%	−0.41%	2.80%
Standard Deviation	6.34%	9.52%	8.46%	7.85%	7.02%	8.46%
No. of Observations	28	16	14	23	42	39
Retail, Food Chains						
Outperformance/Underperformance	1.04%	3.73%	−1.04%	1.42%	0.34%	2.37%
Standard Deviation	6.71%	8.73%	8.56%	8.68%	7.34%	8.66%
No. of Observations	28	16	14	23	42	39
Retail, General Merch.						
Outperformance/Underperformance	−0.74%	0.04%	−1.50%	2.00%	−1.00%	1.21%
Standard Deviation	8.22%	6.65%	9.30%	9.02%	8.49%	8.10%
No. of Observations (3/77–6/96)	27	15	14	22	41	37
Retail, Spec. Apparel						
Outperformance/Underperformance	4.56%	−8.05%	4.14%	5.00%	4.41%	0.25%
Standard Deviation	15.64%	14.13%	16.85%	13.64%	15.69%	14.93%
No. of Observations (6/85–6/96)	15	8	8	14	23	22
Retail Stores, Composite						
Outperformance/Underperformance	−0.18%	−0.29%	−0.61%	2.17%	−0.32%	1.16%
Standard Deviation	6.99%	7.48%	7.61%	7.86%	7.12%	7.70%
No. of Observations	28	16	14	23	42	39
Technology						
Outperformance/Underperformance	3.30%	0.49%	2.20%	−3.41%	2.82%	−1.95%
Standard Deviation	6.80%	7.69%	6.34%	6.25%	6.38%	6.85%
No. of Observations (3/89–6/96)	8	6	6	10	14	16
Telecomm. (Long Distance)						
Outperformance/Underperformance	0.78%	3.25%	1.39%	−3.20%	0.99%	−0.36%
Standard Deviation	9.97%	7.12%	7.89%	7.21%	9.16%	7.74%
No. of Observations (6/84–6/96)	16	11	8	14	24	25
Telephone						
Outperformance/Underperformance	−2.16%	1.47%	−4.25%	2.31%	−2.86%	1.97%
Standard Deviation	7.69%	4.26%	6.96%	5.29%	7.44%	4.85%
No. of Observations	28	16	14	23	42	39
Textiles Apparel						
Outperformance/Underperformance	2.62%	−2.03%	3.10%	0.14%	2.78%	−0.75%
Standard Deviation	8.84%	8.94%	11.86%	10.10%	9.80%	9.58%
No. of Observations	28	16	14	23	42	39
Tobacco						
Outperformance/Underperformance	1.57%	5.49%	−2.65%	3.49%	0.17%	4.31%
Standard Deviation	9.35%	8.60%	8.21%	9.04%	9.11%	8.80%
No. of Observations	28	16	14	23	42	39

Appendix 6.2 *(Continued)*

	Growth above Trend & Rising	Growth above Trend & Falling	Growth below Trend & Rising	Growth below Trend & Falling	Growth Rising	Growth Falling
Transportation						
Outperformance/Underperformance	0.48%	−0.47%	3.05%	−0.93%	1.33%	−0.74%
Standard Deviation	4.55%	4.52%	5.99%	5.59%	5.15%	5.12%
No. of Observations	28	16	14	23	42	39
Truckers						
Outperformance/Underperformance	−4.01%	1.59%	−1.31%	0.76%	−3.11%	1.10%
Standard Deviation	9.07%	12.09%	8.35%	10.23%	8.83%	10.89%
No. of Observations	28	16	14	23	42	39
Trucks & Parts, Heavy Duty						
Outperformance/Underperformance	−0.16%	−0.99%	1.31%	−2.83%	0.33%	−2.08%
Standard Deviation	10.38%	7.60%	7.55%	10.28%	9.46%	9.21%
No. of Observations	28	16	14	23	42	39
Utilities						
Outperformance/Underperformance	−1.91%	0.53%	−3.94%	2.09%	−2.59%	1.47%
Standard Deviation	5.47%	4.16%	7.12%	5.09%	6.07%	4.75%
No. of Observations (6/76–6/96)	32	18	16	27	48	45
Waste Management						
Outperformance/Underperformance	0.48%	2.46%	3.50%	1.51%	1.49%	1.90%
Standard Deviation	9.44%	9.02%	10.65%	9.01%	9.84%	8.91%
No. of Observations	28	16	14	23	42	39

(Quarterly Observations, June 1976–June 1996)*

*All periods June 1976 to June 1996 except as noted. Other periods all end in June 1996, with various start dates as noted.

7   Global Equity Markets

RELATIVE MARKET PERFORMANCE AND THE
GLOBAL ECONOMIC CYCLE

At any given time, the world's economies are at different phases in their
respective business cycles and, as such, their equity markets are at different points in the cycle creating innumerable opportunities and risks
for global investors.

For example, in October 1990, five months before the trough of the
1990–1991 recession in the United States, the U.S. equity market entered a major bull market phase that extended for over six years (see
Exhibit 7.1). The beginning of the market's advance coincided with
the U.S.'s output gap's nearing a trough. For most of 1993 and 1994,
the U.S. equity market basically marked time while the U.S. economy
registered above-trend growth, prompting fears of rising inflation and

Exhibit 7.1   Relative Price Performance of Major Stock Markets (Third Quarter
1990–Third Quarter 1996).

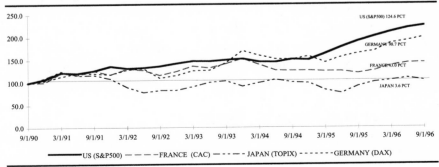

Data Source: Datastream.

attendant increases in interest rates. Not until growth began to moderate to more sustainable levels in 1995 did the market resume its advance on the back of interest rate declines. For the 6-year period from October 7, 1990, to October 8, 1996, the market advanced 124.4 percent. During this period, the U.S. economy grew 12.7 percent in real terms.

The Japanese economy, on the other hand, peaked in 1990 and entered into a period of unprecedented post-World War II weakness. The Japanese equity market mirrored this weakness. The market reached a local peak in March 1991 and did not reach that peak again during the 6-year period represented in Exhibit 7.1. Over the 6-year period from October 1990 to September 1996, the Japanese market (TOPIX) registered a price increase of only 3.6 percent.

In Europe, during the same period, Germany and France closely tracked each other until the early part of 1994. The French equity market then came under severe pressure as long-term French interest rates increased significantly and economic growth in France slipped below potential. The yield on the 10-year bond increased from 5.7 percent to 8.3 percent over the course of the year, and the spread between French and German interest rates moved from parity in January to 65 basis points against France by the end of the year. During 1994, the German market stagnated, but did not sell off despite a backup in interest rates similar to the one experienced in France. Consequently, on a relative basis, the German equity market was more attractive. The German market was supported in the face of rising interest rates by expectations of significant improvement in earnings which were anticipated along with stronger growth. The outlook for the French economy during this period was mixed to negative.

The disparate performance of these four economies and the attendant impact exerted on their equity markets are indicative of the impact that different economic trajectories have on investment market outcomes.

THE RATIONALE FOR INVESTING IN
FOREIGN EQUITY MARKETS

Generally, the rationale for investing in foreign equity markets are the diversification benefits achieved from a portfolio construction standpoint.

Exhibit 7.2 Global Equities Correlation Matrix (1986–1995).

	AUS	CAN	FRA	GER	ITA	JAP	NET	SPA	UK	US
Australia	100.0	65.7	44.0	47.7	27.7	30.2	61.0	52.7	58.3	53.9
Canada		100.0	49.4	46.7	34.1	37.8	69.2	48.6	67.4	75.8
France			100.0	69.5	54.3	39.2	60.9	57.4	58.7	53.4
Germany				100.0	50.5	25.6	71.7	47.5	53.6	46.3
Italy					100.0	41.0	45.6	54.4	38.6	28.3
Japan						100.0	38.6	54.3	35.2	33.0
Netherlands							100.0	56.5	75.5	67.6
Spain								100.0	56.5	51.1
United Kingdom									100.0	76.0
United States										100.0

Data Source: BARRA World Markets Model. Monthly total return data from Morgan Stanley Capital International equity indices. Local market returns.

The different risk, return and correlation properties of different markets make them attractive components of a structured portfolio. Higher expected returns at the same risk level or the same expected returns at a lower risk level can be attained through diversification into multiple markets. Exhibit 7.2 summarizes the correlations of the major global equity markets over the 10-year period from 1986 to 1995, and highlights the different return paths for the major markets.[1]

While diversification is important from a portfolio construction standpoint, the expanded opportunity set in terms of market timing opportunities is also attractive.

GLOBAL BUSINESS CYCLE

Since the seventies, the global business cycle has evolved considerably with the composition and contribution to world growth quite different now.

[1] These correlations are local market returns and are purposely not converted into a common currency to illustrate the divergence of market performance and, hence, the opportunities available. Most investors, wishing to convert international investment returns into their base currency, would look at both local returns and currency impacts for a complete assessment of international investment opportunities.

Exhibit 7.3   Geographical Contribution to World Growth.

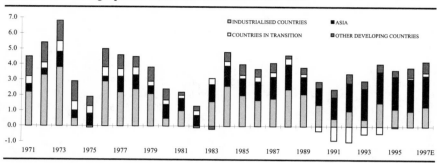

Data Source: BZW Australia Limited. Used with permission of Bill Meischke, Director, Barclays de Zoete Wedd Australia Limited.

According to BZW Securities (Australia), the industrialized countries' share of world output declined from 64 percent in 1970 to 54 percent in 1995. The emerging growth economies of Asia have filled this gap, increasing their share from 11 percent in 1970 to 24 percent in 1995. The outperformance of the Asian economies in terms of relative growth has been and will continue to be reflected in the relative performance of their equity markets. Not only has the contribution to world output from the emerging Asian economies increased, but, according to BZW, their contribution to world growth has grown from minimal levels in the seventies, to become the dominant contribution to growth in the nineties (see Exhibit 7.3).[2]

In the seventies, there was a high degree of correlation between global markets (see Exhibit 7.4).[3] The breakdown of the synchronous path of the major world economies in the early eighties has opened up more opportunities for individual business cycles to enhance global equity returns. Economic divergence, almost by definition, implies equity market divergence.

---

[2] Bill Meischke, BZW Securities, Australia, November 1996. Compiled from IMF data.

[3] The exception was in 1973, when the sharp increase in oil prices impacted the Japanese economy more than other major economies because of Japan's heavy dependence on imported oil. Japan imports more than 90 percent of its energy requirements.

Exhibit 7.4   G-3 Output Gaps.

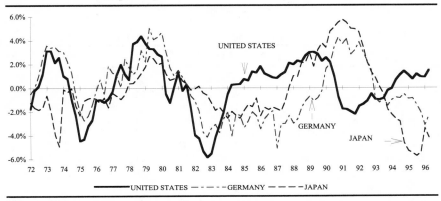

Data Source: Datastream.

The divergence of growth trajectories between economies creates opportunities to time allocations. The investor can focus on the most attractive markets, at any given time, based on the evolution of each of the cycles. Assuming one can forecast, to some degree, or at least glean some insights into the evolution of the cycles, the incremental returns available are substantial.

Global Linkages and Capital Market Integration

Individual country cycles are linked to the global business cycle on multiple levels. The most obvious link is through trade. (See Exhibit 7.5.) As one might expect, given the European Economic Union, the European economies are the most open, with exports comprising 22.5 percent of nominal GDP and imports comprising 21.8 percent.[4] Most of the trade is intra-European: 68.5 percent of European exports are destined for other European countries. Within Europe, the importance of trade varies. For Germany and France, exports of goods and services account for 37.8 percent and 26.4 percent of GDP, respectively. The Dutch economy is

---

[4] Organization for Economic Cooperation and Development, *OECD Economic Outlook,* June 1996, Annex Table 64.

Exhibit 7.5   Geographical Structure of OECD Trade.

	(Percentage of Nominal GDP)							
	Source of Imports				Destination of Exports			
Source/Destination	1962	1972	1982	1994	1962	1972	1982	1994
USA								
OECD	1.84	3.47	4.91	6.51	2.22	2.94	4.18	5.23
Europe	0.78	1.27	1.65	1.96	1.09	1.25	1.89	1.77
North America	0.74	1.37	1.97	2.68	0.81	1.19	1.44	2.48
Other	0.31	0.84	1.29	1.86	0.33	0.49	0.84	0.97
Non-OECD	1.02	1.12	2.83	3.48	1.55	1.18	2.56	2.48
DAEs +China	0.08	0.33	0.87	2.02	0.11	0.22	0.67	1.21
OPEC	0.26	0.22	0.99	0.50	0.18	0.23	0.73	0.29
Europe								
OECD	11.38	13.56	17.81	17.53	10.29	13.25	16.85	18.05
Europe	8.61	11.22	14.50	14.62	8.48	11.22	14.59	15.39
North America	2.22	1.73	2.41	1.87	1.36	1.66	1.81	1.98
Other	0.55	0.61	0.90	1.04	0.45	0.38	0.46	0.67
Non-OECD	4.20	3.79	6.30	4.22	3.43	3.25	5.65	4.43
DAEs +China	0.23	0.27	0.61	1.24	0.25	0.26	0.46	1.18
OPEC	1.16	1.33	2.77	0.66	0.54	0.59	2.08	0.62
Japan								
OECD	5.37	3.99	4.41	2.89	3.94	5.23	6.22	4.46
Europe	1.00	0.82	0.93	0.94	1.11	1.57	2.01	1.43
North America	3.60	2.37	2.77	1.60	2.56	3.36	3.71	2.81
Other	0.77	0.80	0.72	0.34	0.27	0.29	0.50	0.22
Non-OECD	3.88	3.72	7.67	3.10	4.13	4.17	6.49	4.16
DAEs +China	0.84	0.73	1.61	1.63	1.29	1.67	2.39	3.03
OPEC	1.12	1.50	4.45	0.83	0.52	0.61	2.00	0.36

DAEs: Dynamic Asian Economies (Taiwan, Hong Kong, Korea, Malaysia, Thailand, and Singapore.)

Data Source: Organization for Economic Cooperation and Development, *OECD Economic Outlook,* June 1996, Annex Table 64.

more open; exports of goods and services account for 59.4 percent of GDP and imports of goods and services account for some 52.8 percent of GDP.[5]

The U.S. economy is significantly less open. Exports comprise only 7.7 percent of nominal GDP, and fully 32.2 percent of those exports go to Canada. The Japanese economy is slightly more open than the U.S.

[5] International Financial Statistics, International Monetary Fund, Washington, DC: October, 1996.

economy. Exports comprise 8.6 percent of nominal GDP. Thirty-five percent of Japan's exports go to the Dynamic Asian Economies (DAEs) and China, while only 27 percent of Japan's imports originate from that region. Japan's trade imbalance in recent years has been considerable, with exports outweighing imports. This persistent imbalance has prompted major capital outflows so that Japan has become the major creditor to the world.

The greater the openness of an economy, the more closely linked that economy's performance will be to its major trading partners. The openness of the European economies, combined with the customs and monetary union, often causes this regional group to move in tandem. When they do not move in sync, the stress is generally manifest in exchange rate pressure within the European Exchange Rate Mechanism (ERM) and/or via interest rate volatility. This has been particularly true with the French economy. France's *forte* franc policy and tenacious support of the franc over recent years has kept interest rates higher in France than has been warranted by inflation and domestic economic conditions.

The integration of the European economies is manifest by the fairly close correlations among European equity markets, shown in the correlation matrix presented in Exhibit 7.6. Even though the European economies are highly integrated, periodic divergences offer considerable opportunities for asset shifts between markets. The core European

Exhibit 7.6 European Equity Markets Correlation Matrix.

	BEL	DEN	FIN	FRA	GER	ITA	NET	NOR	SPA	SWE	SWI	UK
					(1988–1996)							
Belgium	100.0	50.2	32.7	68.2	62.9	46.9	69.4	48.9	51.2	39.2	52.2	49.6
Denmark		100.0	37.0	44.7	56.1	46.4	55.0	51.0	52.0	48.8	48.8	44.5
Finland			100.0	29.3	38.2	48.4	49.2	52.6	52.3	53.6	33.5	43.3
France				100.0	71.7	45.8	64.8	45.3	51.9	41.4	56.2	58.1
Germany					100.0	53.3	65.3	48.0	48.4	46.2	57.5	50.6
Italy						100.0	50.8	44.1	51.4	40.3	41.4	40.2
Netherlands							100.0	65.2	60.7	54.2	66.6	75.1
Norway								100.0	48.7	52.3	45.5	55.5
Spain									100.0	69.1	55.0	53.0
Sweden										100.0	49.0	49.6
Switzerland											100.0	65.2
U.K.												100.0

Data Source: BARRA World Markets Model. Monthly total return data from Morgan Stanley Capital International Equity Indices.

markets—Germany, France, the Netherlands and Belgium—are highly correlated with each other, as are the Scandinavian markets of Sweden, Finland, Denmark and Norway.

The increasingly free mobility of capital on a global basis has added significantly to global integration. The dismantling of capital market barriers over the past decade and a half has significantly increased the mobility and magnitude of capital movement. This mobility, in turn, has lessened local central bank control of individual capital markets and has increased individual market sensitivity to global market developments.

For example, during the 1994 bond market sell off, the lack of liquidity in some of the small, high-yield markets, where hedge funds and other leveraged players had large positions, forced market participants to hedge their exposure in these markets by establishing short positions in other markets with greater liquidity. The markets used as hedge markets then sold off more than would have been the case in the past. Another example is the heavy dependence of the United States on foreign capital to fund the pernicious federal deficit. Absent large capital flows from surplus countries such as Japan, U.S. interest rates would have been measurably higher than they have been during the past decade.

Global capital flows are often the driving force behind equity market moves as global investors engage in market timing to enhance returns. Small shifts in country allocation levels by U.S. pension and mutual funds can result in major capital inflows or outflows in some of the smaller capitalization markets and can cause pronounced price moves.

MONITORING GLOBAL, REGIONAL AND INDIVIDUAL COUNTRY BUSINESS CYCLES

The same framework that is useful for evaluating the U.S. business cycle can be used to evaluate other countries' economic cycles and the global business cycle. The output gap; productivity; labor costs; inflation; monetary policy, liquidity and the growth of the monetary aggregates and exchange rate movements—all are important variables that should be assessed when evaluating the global cycle and the relative performance of individual economies. All of these variables can be aggregated on a weighted basis to determine global trends and patterns.

Exhibit 7.7   OECD Output Gap and Inflation (CPI).

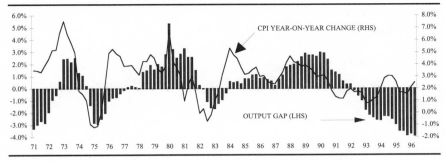

Data Source: Datastream.

Equity Markets, Interest Rates and the Profit Cycle

The two main drivers of equity markets are interest rates and profits. They are both set by the business cycle through the interaction of growth and inflation.

The importance of the global growth cycle's relation to inflation is clearly evident from the correlation between the output gap and year-on-year changes in consumer prices (see Exhibit 7.7). During periods when the global economy is growing above its long-term potential, capacity constraints emerge in capital and labor markets, prompting inflationary pressures.[6] Historically, there has been a somewhat asymmetric relationship between inflation and growth, with inflation more sensitive and responsive to upward pressure than to downward pressure. This is because workers are more sensitive to nominal wage levels than to real wages. Workers aggressively resist downward adjustments to nominal wages during periods of economic weakness, thus circumscribing deflation on the downside. This asymmetry makes it difficult for corporations to rationalize wage costs during periods of slack.

This phenomenon was clearly evident from 1992 to 1996. Despite a very large negative output gap within the OECD region, deflation was limited. The deflation that occurred was evident primarily in Japan. The potential for deflation in Europe is quite limited, even during periods of

[6] The aggregate real growth trend for the OECD economies, from 1970 to IIQ 1996, was 2.9 percent.

pronounced weakness, given worker militancy and the overly generous social support system.

During periods of strong economic growth and high-capacity utilization levels, unit labor costs closely track economywide inflation as measured by the CPI. During periods of high inflation, workers aggressively push for nominal wage increases commensurate with headline inflation. The workers' focus is on nominal as opposed to real wages during these periods.

This behavior has significant implications for corporate profits. During periods of economic weakness and moderating or declining inflation, nominal wages are "sticky" on the downside, thereby artificially keeping the wages bill higher than is warranted by real output. Rather than adjust employee compensation, corporations bear this either in the form of lower margins or by laying off workers.

The impact of the global business cycle on inflation—and, in turn, on interest rates—is critical when evaluating the prospects for global equities. All else being equal, an expanding or positive output gap portends rising inflation and interest rates and a contracting or negative output gap implies falling inflation and interest rates.

The variability of the profit cycle, both globally and locally, is captured by changes in the level of industrial production. The OECD leading indicator series, which includes global, regional and country series, is a good leading indicator to monitor for turning points and the direction of industrial production. In general, changes in the leading indicators on a year-over-year basis lead year-over-year changes in industrial production by one to two quarters (Exhibit 7.8). The leading indicators are fairly reliable advance indicators of swings in profits around their trend growth levels.

Monetary Policy Cycle and the Monetary Aggregates

The monetary policy cycle is extremely important for investment markets. A typical cycle unfolds as follows. Economic growth falls below potential, creating a significant output gap and an attendant abatement of inflation. This slack prompts the monetary authorities to loosen policy by adding liquidity to the system. This loosening generally takes the

Exhibit 7.8 OECD Leading Indicators and Industrial Production.

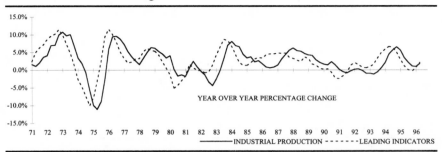

Data Source: Datastream.

form of money creation, which prompts growth in the relevant monetary aggregates to move above the growth rate of nominal GDP. This establishes the monetary preconditions for renewed growth (Exhibit 7.9). The availability of cheap money and credit, at this point in the cycle, tends to drive asset markets as excess liquidity flows into financial assets. As growth resumes, liquidity is increasingly absorbed in real activity. When economic growth inevitably moves above a sustainable level, inflation reemerges and the monetary authorities begin to apply the brakes by increasing interest rates and slowing the rate of money growth. The subsequent slowing of the economy is followed by policy easing, which marks the beginning of the next cycle.[7] This ebb and flow of excess liquidity is an important factor determining market behavior.

REGIONAL AND COUNTRY CYCLES

Regional economic groups and individual countries' economies possess unique characteristics that are worth considering in some detail when

---

[7] Many of the linkages between the monetary aggregates and the economy have broken down over the past decade, following significant financial market innovation. The break in these links has prompted the Federal Reserve to abandon targeting growth of the monetary aggregates, to focus more attention on other indicators, and to target the level of interest rates. Despite the Fed's deemphasis of the monetary aggregates, they remain important in other economies and consequently bear monitoring.

Exhibit 7.9   OECD Money Supply (M1) Growth.

14.0%
12.0%
10.0%
8.0%
6.0%   YEAR-OVER-YEAR PERCENTAGE CHANGE
4.0%
2.0%
      81   82   83   84   85   86   87   88   89   90   91   92   93   94   95   96   97

Data Source: Datastream.

evaluating prospects for their equity markets and the links between their
economies and market performance.

Continental Europe

The continental European economic cycle is dominated by Germany,
France and, to a lesser extent, Italy. The integration and linkages attributable to the European Union (EU) and European Monetary Union
(EMU) are fostering increasing synchronization among the member
economies.

The European leading indicators generated by the OECD (Exhibit 7.10)
have proved fairly reliable for assessing turning points in the European

Exhibit 7.10   European Leading Indicators and Industrial Production (U.K., Germany, France and Italy).

15%
10%
5%
0%
-5%
-10%   YEAR OVER YEAR PERCENTAGE CHANGE
-15%
      71 72 73 74 75 76 77 78 79 80 81 82 83 84 85 86 87 88 89 90 91 92 93 94 95 96

————INDUSTRIAL PRODUCTION - - - - - -LEADING INDICATORS

Data Source: Datastream.

economy and the direction of industrial production, which is often the key to swings in the profit cycle.

The Exchange Rate Mechanism (ERM), which sets bands of deviation among the member currencies, forces significant monetary discipline on the member countries. This discipline has helped to bring about an unprecedented level of convergence of inflation and interest rates among the member countries. Moreover, the Maastricht treaty imposes constraints on government debt and deficit levels as a percentage of GDP, which will foster a further convergence of economic policy and performance within the region.

Germany and France are the linchpins of the system and both are highly committed at the political level to making monetary union work. The increasingly tight relationship between long-term interest rates in the two economies (Exhibit 7.11) is clear evidence of the countries' commitment to policy coordination and cooperation.

The convergence of inflation and interest rates between Germany and France has heightened the importance of relative growth as the dominant factor in determining the relative performance of the two equity markets. This is clearly evident from the two graphs in Exhibits 7.12 and 7.13 which show, respectively, the relative performance of the two equity markets over the period from July 1987 to August 1996, and the relative performance of the two economies as represented by deviations from trend growth.

Exhibit 7.11   French and German 10-Year Bond Yields.

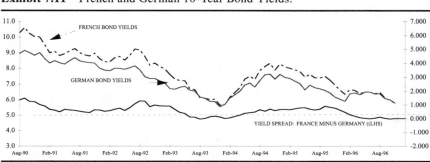

Data Source: Datastream.

Exhibit 7.12   Relative Performance of French and German Equities.

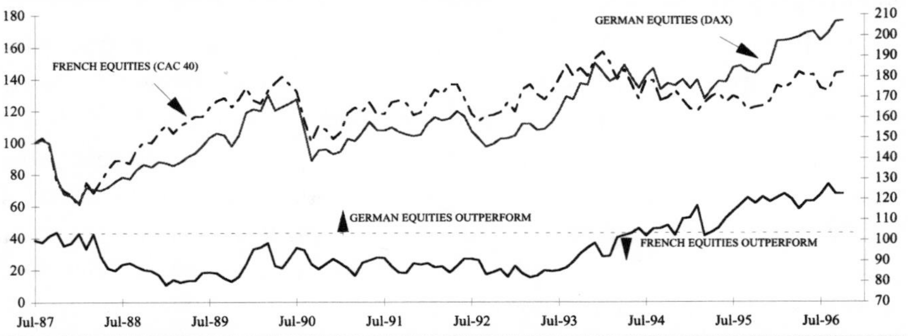

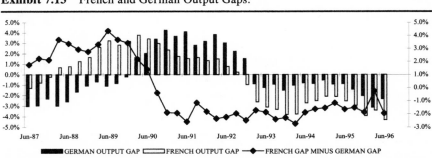

Data Source: Datastream.

The French equity market outperformed the German equity market from mid-1987 to early 1989. The German economy underperformed and registered sub-par growth relative both to Germany's potential and relative to France. By early 1989, however, the German output gap had begun to close, and the German economy moved to a period of above-trend growth that began in the first quarter of 1990 and lasted until early 1993. As the German economy moved from a position of significant excess capacity—as represented by the negative output gap—to a position of fully utilized capacity, corporate profits and expectations of profits rose and the German stock market began to track the French stock market, which had outperformed earlier in response to a closure of the output gap. Following this "catch-up" period in late 1989 and early 1990,

Exhibit 7.13   French and German Output Gaps.

Data Source: Datastream.

Germany and France alternated the leadership position. The French equity market outpaced the German market in the second half of 1990.

For most of 1990, 1991 and 1992, both economies registered above-trend growth and parallel interest rate moves, which resulted in the two markets basically tracking each other. In early 1993, growth flagged in both economies. The French economy significantly underperformed the German economy on both an absolute and a relative basis (see Exhibit 7.13). The pronounced weakness in the French economy relative to Germany resulted in a significant outperformance of German equities relative to French equities as corporate profits and forward profit expectations in Germany held up better than profits in France.

As monetary convergence within the EMU countries continues, the relative position of each country within the business cycle will become ever more important for extracting incremental excess returns from Europe.

Continental Europe accounts for roughly 20 percent of the global equity market on a capitalization basis.

The United Kingdom

Approximately 10 percent of the world's equity market is accounted for by U.K. equities.

The stock market in the U.K., like other major markets, drives off interest rates and the corporate profit cycle. The fundamental backdrop for interest rates and profits is the performance of the economy relative to its long-term potential. In this regard, the U.K. has registered real growth of 2.0 percent over the past 26 years with periods of significant deviation from this trend, as reflected in the output gap shown in Exhibit 7.15.

During periods when the economy has been operating above its long-term growth potential, inflationary pressures have emerged, ultimately prompting a monetary policy response with attendant increases in interest rates. The two major spikes in inflation over the past three decades were triggered by the quadrupling of oil prices in 1973 and 1979 (Exhibit 7.16).

The corporate profit cycle is heavily dependent on the economic cycle and on changes in industrial production. Exhibit 7.17 depicts

Exhibit 7.14   U.K. Equity Market (Rolling 12-Month Price Performance).

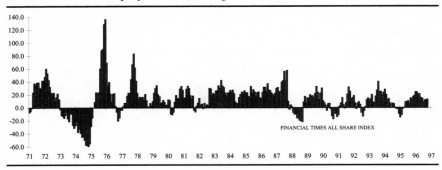

Data Source: Datastream.

Exhibit 7.15   U.K. Output Gap.

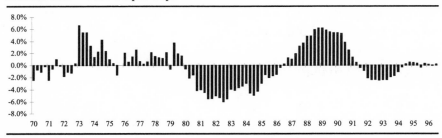

Data Source: Datastream.

Exhibit 7.16   U.K. GDP Price Deflator (Year-on-Year Percentage Change).

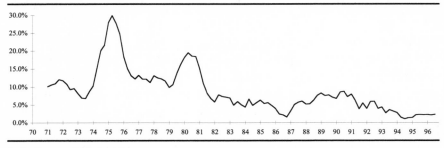

Data Source: Datastream.

Exhibit 7.17 U.K. Industrial Production and Real Corporate Profits.

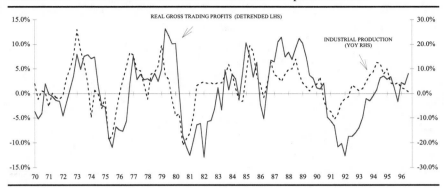

Data Source: Datastream.

year-over-year changes in industrial production and in real corporate profits around their long-term trend.[8] Turning points in industrial production tend to lead turning points in real corporate profits by several quarters on a year-over-year basis. Over the 26-year period shown, gross nominal profits averaged 11.0 percent and real profits averaged 2.1 percent.

Often, the CBI business confidence indicator, produced by the Confederation of British Industry, gives an indication of the direction of industrial production and of corporate profits (Exhibit 7.18).

Japan

The artificial nature of Japan's financial markets is well documented. Speculative bubbles in both the property and equity markets over recent decades have caused a rigorous assessment of the linkages between economic fundamentals and asset markets to be fraught with difficulty. The problem is further complicated by the predilection of Japanese bureaucrats to interfere with market forces and artificially prop up prices. The constraints imposed on property transactions in the early nineties and the artificial support afforded banks and savings associations in the

---

[8] Gross trading profits of companies and financial institutions were deflated by the GDP price deflator and then detrended to show the sensitivity of the profit cycle to the economic cycle, as represented by year-by-year changes in industrial production.

Exhibit 7.18   U.K. CBI Business Confidence Indicator and Industrial Production.

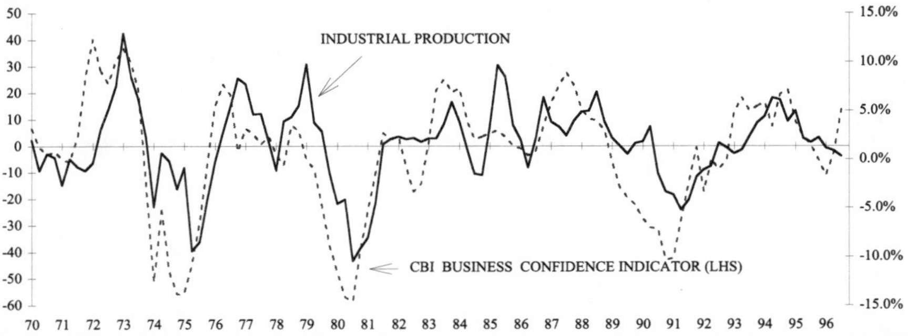

Data Source: Datastream.

mid-nineties are two prominent examples of how bureaucratic interference with market forces has resulted in artificially maintained asset prices. The official price keeping operations (PKO) conducted in 1994 and 1995, whereby retirement savings institutions such as the Postal Savings Plan were periodically directed to support the market by buying shares with member funds, is a classic example of official intervention.

Despite these impediments, fundamental business cycle factors do affect and drive the Japanese equity market. As with the other markets, the level and direction of the economy play a key role in the earnings outlook and interest rates factor heavily as a benchmark for alternative investments.

The impact of the exchange rate on the Japanese market is considerable given the importance of export earnings for such key sectors of the Japanese economy as autos and electronics. A depreciating yen results in increased price competitiveness and translation gains on foreign source earnings and is generally positive for the market. Yen appreciation tends to result in an initial margin squeeze as exporters endeavor to maintain market share by "wearing" the impact of a stronger yen. Historically, however, corporate Japan has been remarkably good at accommodating an appreciating yen.

Sentiment, government intentions and market momentum should all be weighed more heavily in the Japanese equity market than in other markets when assessing the market outlook.

Exhibit 7.19   Japanese Equity market (TOPIX).

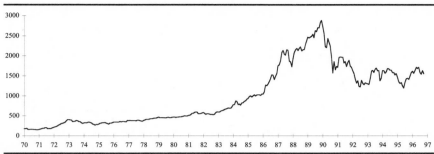

Data Source: Datastream.

The Japanese market accounts for approximately 20 percent of the global equity market. The weight of the Japanese market has diminished considerably following the collapse of equity prices in the early nineties.

Emerging Markets and High-Growth Economies

The expanding share of GDP taken by the emerging growth economies combined with their increasing importance in driving world growth makes the equity markets of Southeast Asia, Latin America and Eastern Europe extremely attractive. These markets offer both high returns and high risk.

The high-growth economies bring together a confluence of factors that provide exceptional opportunities and risks. The driving force behind these markets is a combination of high savings and capital investment and an underutilization of labor. Improvement in the skill set of labor through education and training, combined with increasing investments in capital is creating explosive growth prospects in countries such as Korea, Taiwan, Singapore, Thailand and Malaysia. There comes a point where unutilized capacity begins to diminish and the marginal output generated from the input of additional capital diminishes and growth slows.

The low-growth regimes of the industrialized countries reflect the limitations on the potential for labor force growth and for increased productivity. Growth is limited to modest levels when compared with the

Exhibit 7.20   Relative Price Performance of High Growth Markets.

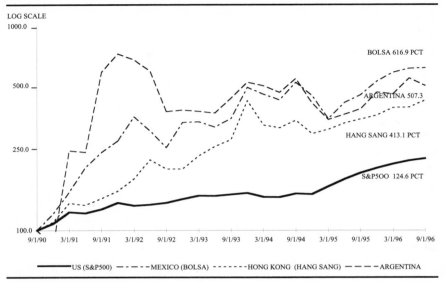

Data Source: Bloomberg.

real growth rates of between 6 and 10 percent that are prevalent in the emerging growth economies. Indeed, the potential for continued very high growth in countries such as China, Vietnam and Eastern Europe is clearly in place. This growth is what makes these equity markets potentially attractive. One should not, however, discount the potential for major policy mistakes, which can derail economies and markets in these countries.

The emerging growth economies are linked with and leveraged into the major economies. Consequently, they often react severely to developments in the major economies. For example, the Hong Kong equity and property markets react, on a leveraged basis, to changes in U.S. interest rates, given the peg of the Hong Kong dollar to the U.S. dollar. Countries such as Singapore and Malaysia, which are heavily influenced by the demand for semiconductors in the United States, react sharply to changes in demand.

8 Seasonality in Global Equity Markets

Stock markets exhibit strong seasonal tendencies that can be exploited to significantly enhance market timing. Exceptionally strong and persistent seasonal patterns are evident in Italy, Sweden and Singapore, and strong, albeit somewhat weaker patterns are evident in the United States, the United Kingdom, Spain and Hong Kong. The other major markets exhibit statistically significant seasonality in some months, but, in general, their overall patterns are weak and statistically insignificant.

The strength in most equity markets around the turn of the year is one of the most pronounced and regular annual patterns. August, September, October and November are habitually weak months across most equity markets, with substantial underperformance evident. Almost without exception, June is also a very weak month in most markets.

Seasonal patterns are prompted by numerous factors that differ from market to market. From an investment perspective, it is important to understand the factors that underpin seasonal variation to ensure that the factors that have caused seasonality in the past remain in place and, as such, are meaningful considerations in making investment decisions.

When considering seasonal effects and their potential impact on investment strategies, it is important to consider not only seasonal patterns, but also the degree of confidence associated with those patterns. The probability-adjusted expected excess returns and total excess returns for the 10-year period from 1986 to 1995 are presented in Exhibits 8.2, 8.6 and 8.9 for each region considered.

SEASONALITY IN THE ANGLO-SAXON
EQUITY MARKETS

The "January effect" in the U.S. equity market is well known and has been documented extensively in investment literature.[1] While the academic literature that explores this phenomenon does not give a definitive explanation, it is widely accepted in investment circles that the effect is the result of end-of-year tax loss selling, particularly of small capitalization stocks with investors then reinvesting the proceeds early in the new calendar/tax year, causing a market rally. Although there is evidence of "front-loading" in recent years creating a December-January effect, the timing of the phenomenon nevertheless remains an important force in the U.S. equity market. Some academics argue that market knowledge of tax loss selling would prompt an adjustment in financial markets, altering the demand/supply conditions and thus eliminating the effect. The argument is: If market participants understand the phenomenon, they will adjust to take advantage of the effect and will thereby eliminate it. The counter to this argument is that the effect persists and remains "unexplained" by other theories.

Over the 10-year period from 1986 to 1995, the U.S. stock market registered excess returns of 4.5 percent per annum from December to February. That is, capital appreciation in the U.S. equity market, using the Morgan Stanley Capital International Index of price returns, has been 8.2 percent over this 3-month period, compared with a normal capital appreciation of 3.5 percent for an average 3-month period. The excess return in January alone has been 1.73 percent over this period, and there has been a 97 percent probability of occurrence (see Exhibit 8.11). The January or turn-of-the-year effect is a powerful seasonal phenomenon.

---

[1] See, for example, Michael S. Rozeff and William R. Kinney, Jr., "Capital Market Seasonality: The Case of Stock Returns," *Journal of Financial Economics, 3,* No. 4 (October 1976): pp. 379–402; and Robert A. Ariel, "A Monthly Effect in Stock Returns," *Journal of Financial Economics, 18,* No. 1 (March 1987): pp. 161–174. The case against a January effect is made by Jay R. Ritter and Navin Chopra, in "Portfolio Rebalancing and the Turn-of-the-Year Effect," *Journal of Finance, 44,* No. 1 (March 1989): pp. 149–166.

April and May appear to have tax-related seasonal tendencies. April generally registers sub-par returns because investors are paying tax liabilities. May exhibits above-par returns as tax refunds get channeled into the market.

As Exhibit 8.1 demonstrates, August, September, October and November are often weak months in the U.S. stock market. September and October registered the most persistent weakness from 1986 to 1995. This pattern held true for Canada, the United Kingdom and Australia. (See the table of probability adjusted returns in Exhibit 8.2.)

Canada and Australia—markets that are heavily represented by resource stocks—possess similar patterns. Both markets exhibit strong seasonal performance in March and May in response to seasonally strong commodity prices in these months. In Australia, tax loss selling is pronounced in June, (the end of their financial year) and the proceeds are reinvested in July. This activity results in a weak June and a strong July.

The strong seasonal patterns in the resource sector of the Australian stock market are shown in Exhibit 8.3. The patterns suggest an overweight to resources during the period from March to May, heavy overweight in July, and then an underweight in resource stocks and the entire market from August to November.

Based on observed seasonal patterns over the past decade, the most promising investment or timing strategies for the Anglo-Saxon markets

Exhibit 8.1 Seasonality in the Anglo-Saxon Equity Markets, 1986–1995.

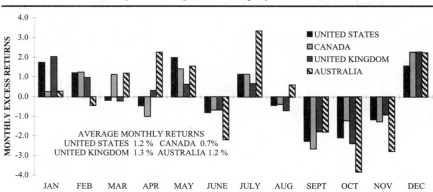

Exhbit 8.2 Probability Adjusted Expected Returns.*

	Jan	Feb	Mar	Apr	May	June	July	Aug	Sep	Oct	Nov	Dec
United States												
Confidence Level	97%	80%	67%	43%	52%	58%	47%	40%	95%	93%	33%	21%
Expected Excess Return	1.67	0.96	-0.12	-0.2	1.03	-0.47	0.53	-0.18	-2.16	-1.97	-0.39	0.33
Expected Total Return	2.83	2.12	1.04	0.96	2.19	0.69	1.69	0.98	-1	-0.81	0.77	1.49
Canada												
Confidence Level	75%	20%	25%	50%	39%	48%	6%	41%	91%	90%	39%	68%
Expected Excess Return	0.19	0.25	0.28	-0.51	0.54	-0.32	0.06	-0.16	-2.42	-1.11	-0.51	1.53
Expected Total Return	0.86	0.92	0.95	0.16	1.21	0.35	0.73	0.51	-1.75	-0.44	0.16	2.2
United Kingdom												
Confidence Level	99%	84%	73%	49%	96%	93%	88%	64%	97%	98%	77%	55%
Expected Excess Return	2.01	0.82	-0.17	0.16	0.59	-0.63	0.58	-0.46	-1.75	-2.35	-0.72	1.25
Expected Total Return	3.26	2.07	1.08	1.41	1.84	0.62	1.83	0.79	-0.5	-1.1	0.53	2.5
Australia												
Confidence Level	83%	82%	10%	72%	11%	85%	59%	32%	59%	89%	85%	48%
Expected Excess Return	0.23	-0.38	0.12	1.63	0.17	-1.87	1.96	0.19	-1.07	-3.45	-2.38	1.08
Expected Total Return	1.42	0.81	1.31	2.82	1.36	-0.68	3.15	1.38	0.12	-2.26	-1.19	2.27

*Excess and total returns are adjusted by the probability of occurrence.

Data Source: Morgan Stanley Capital International.

Exhibit 8.3 Seasonality in the Australian Stock Market, 1985–1995.

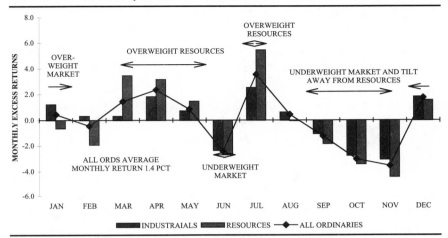

are listed in Exhibit 8.4. In the U.S. equity market, for example, by being long or overweight in December, January and February, one would expect 300 basis points of excess return for a total return of 6.6 percent for the 3-month period, compared to a normal return of 1.16 percent per month or 3.5 percent for an average 3-month period. Over the period from August to November, the market has underperformed by 430 basis points, yielding an expected return of only 1.93 percent for the 4-month period.

Exhibit 8.4 Investment Strategies Suggested by Past Seasonal Patterns.

	Monthly Avg. Capital Appreciation	Long/Overweight			Short/Underweight		
		Open	Close	Expected Excess Return*	Open	Close	Expected Excess Return*
United States	1.16%	Dec	Feb	3.0%	Aug	Nov	−4.3%
Canada	0.67%	Dec	Mar	2.3%	Aug	Nov	−4.2%
United Kingdom	1.25%	Dec	Feb	4.1%	Aug	Nov	−5.2%
Australia	1.19%	Dec	May	2.9%	Sept	Nov	−6.8%

*Excess and total returns are adjusted by the probability of occurrence, and refer only to capital returns, not to total returns.

SEASONALITY IN THE CONTINENTAL EUROPEAN EQUITY MARKETS

In general terms, Continental European seasonal patterns have been broadly consistent with the patterns in the major Anglo-Saxon markets. December to April has been a strong period (Germany and France marginally underperformed in January), and August to November have been marked by underperformance, as is evident in Exhibit 8.5.

Italy and Sweden have had very pronounced seasonal patterns, and these patterns have occurred with very high probabilities as is clear from Exhibit 8.6 which sets out the probabilities and the probability-adjusted expected excess returns. Seasonal patterns in Germany and France have been much less certain than those evident in Italy and Sweden.

Italy and Sweden appear to offer the most promising gains from seasonal timing. In the Italian stock market, the period from December to April has been seasonally strong with expected excess returns of 12.4 percent indicated by past performance, for a total return of 15.8 percent for the five-month period. By avoiding exposure from August to November, 9.6 percent of underperformance could have been avoided in the past.

Exhibit 8.5   Seasonality in the Continental European Equity Markets, 1986–1995.

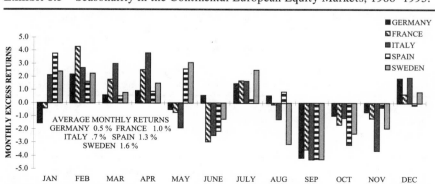

Exhibit 8.6 Probability Adjusted Return Expectations.*

	Jan	Feb	Mar	Apr	May	June	July	Aug	Sep	Oct	Nov	Dec
Germany												
Confidence Level	2%	63%	58%	64%	18%	59%	45%	42%	34%	6%	24%	77%
Expected Excess Return	-0.04	1.36	0.33	0.58	-0.09	0.33	0.66	0.23	-1.43	-0.06	-0.17	1.43
Expected Total Return	0.48	1.88	0.85	1.10	0.43	0.85	1.18	0.75	-0.91	0.46	0.35	1.95
France												
Confidence Level	75%	53%	25%	55%	56%	85%	17%	41%	60%	69%	33%	7%
Expected Excess Return	-0.31	2.26	0.45	1.38	-0.41	-2.52	0.28	-0.05	-2.13	-1.15	-0.39	0.04
Expected Total Return	0.64	3.21	1.40	2.33	0.54	-1.57	1.23	0.90	-1.18	-0.20	0.56	0.99
Italy												
Confidence Level	100%	69%	90%	91%	98%	99%	88%	75%	99%	99%	99%	91%
Expected Excess Return	2.10	1.83	2.68	3.46	-1.87	-2.46	1.45	-0.93	-4.25	-1.12	-3.58	1.74
Expected Total Return	2.84	2.57	3.42	4.20	-1.13	-1.72	2.19	-0.19	-3.51	-0.38	-2.84	2.48
Spain												
Confidence Level	95%	18%	41%	52%	6%	80%	76%	66%	98%	93%	74%	81%
Expected Excess Return	3.55	0.28	0.21	0.44	0.14	-1.72	0.20	0.55	-4.14	-2.96	-0.25	-0.15
Expected Total Return	4.87	1.60	1.53	1.76	1.46	-0.40	1.52	1.87	-2.82	-1.64	1.07	1.17
Sweden												
Confidence Level	99%	43%	79%	73%	83%	95%	30%	99%	99%	93%	76%	70%
Expected Excess Return	2.37	0.95	0.61	1.09	2.56	-1.17	0.75	-3.10	-4.22	-2.18	-1.48	0.58
Expected Total Return	3.92	2.50	2.16	2.64	4.11	0.38	2.30	-1.55	-2.67	-0.63	0.07	2.13

*Excess and total returns are adjusted by the probability of occurrence.

Data Source: Morgan Stanley Capital International.

Exhibit 8.7   Investment Strategies Suggested by Past Seasonal Patterns.

	Monthly Avg. Capital Appreciation	Long/Overweight			Short/Underweight		
		Open	Close	Expected Excess Return*	Open	Close	Expected Excess Return*
Germany	0.52%	Dec	Apr	3.7%	Sept	Nov	−1.7%
France	0.95%	Feb	Apr	4.1%	Aug	Nov	−3.7%
Italy	0.74%	Dec	Apr	12.4%	Aug	Nov	−9.6%
Spain	1.32%	Jan	May	4.7%	Sept	Nov	−7.2%
Sweden	1.55%	Dec	May	8.4%	Aug	Nov	−10.6%

*Excess and total returns are adjusted by the probability of occurrence, and they refer only to capital returns, not to total returns.

Sweden offers similar, albeit less dramatic opportunities. The expected excess performance for the December to May period is 8.4 percent, and the underperformance from August to November is 10.6 percent.

There is little to be gained from seasonal timing in the German market (see Exhibit 8.7). France and Spain both offer expected gains from early-year outperformance, followed by weakness in the fall.

SEASONALITY IN THE ASIAN EQUITY MARKETS

An important factor in the seasonal pattern observed in the Southeast Asian markets is the Chinese lunar new year, which occurs in late January or early February. Often, the period preceding the new year is a strong period in Hong Kong, Singapore and Malaysia (Exhibit 8.8). Occasionally, the month immediately following is also strong. As in most other equity markets, August through November is a period of sub-par returns in the Asian markets.

In Japan, the fiscal year ends in March, but the market shows no statistical evidence of a year-end effect. Other than the September-through-November weakness, January and June are the only other

Exhibit 8.8   Seasonality in the Asian Equity Markets, 1986–1995.

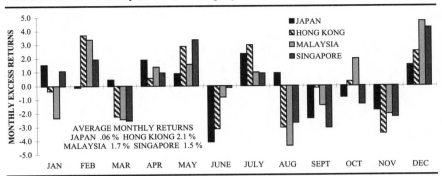

months that exhibit significant seasonal patterns. January has registered excess returns and June has been sharply negative.

As is evident from Exhibit 8.8 and Exhibit 8.9, seasonal weakness in Hong Kong and Singapore has been pronounced and statistically significant from August to November.

When considering any investment strategy from a seasonal perspective, the possibility of achieving excess returns or avoiding excess losses must be weighed against the costs of executing the strategy, the probability of occurrence and the opportunity cost associated with the strategy. In the more volatile Asian markets, it is particularly important to consider all of these factors before making an investment decision (Exhibit 8.10).

Exhibit 8.11 maps the seasonal patterns for the major equity markets over the 10-year period from 1986 to 1995. Regression analysis using dummy variables was employed to determine seasonal variations for each month for each of the countries. The returns listed represent only price changes and not total returns. In addition to the excess returns observed for each month, the t statistic was used to establish a confidence level for each month. The confidence level appears in parentheses in Exhibit 8.11.

Exhibit 8.9 Probability Adjusted Returns Expectations.*

	Jan	Feb	Mar	Apr	May	June	July	Aug	Sep	Oct	Nov	Dec
Japan												
Confidence Level	90%	66%	25%	0%	63%	90%	51%	9%	88%	75%	82%	49%
Expected Excess Return	1.38	-0.09	0.11	0	0.55	-3.69	1.17	0.08	-2.09	-0.63	-1.46	0.74
Expected Total Return	2.02	0.55	0.75	0.64	1.19	-3.05	1.81	0.72	-1.45	0.01	-0.82	1.38
Hong Kong												
Confidence Level	98%	64%	97%	46%	57%	84%	51%	90%	97%	60%	94%	24%
Expected Excess Return	-0.37	2.37	-2.18	0.25	1.63*	-2.65*	1.51	-2.73	-0.16	0.19	-3.29	0.59
Expected Total Return	1.77	4.51	-0.04	2.39	3.77*	-0.51*	3.65	-0.59	1.98	2.33	-1.15	2.73
Malaysia												
Confidence Level	20%	86%	3%	68%	70%	32%	63%	43%	19%	75%	6%	93%
Expected Excess Return	-0.46	2.91	-0.06	0.92	1.09	-0.27	0.61	-1.87	-0.28	1.47	-0.12	4.35
Expected Total Return	1.22	4.59	1.62	2.6	2.77	1.41	2.29	-0.19	1.4	3.15	1.56	6.03
Singapore												
Confidence Level	99%	78%	98%	19%	57%	84%	93%	96%	98%	92%	96%	43%
Expected Excess Return	1.05	1.49	-2.51	0.18	1.9	-0.12	0.84	-2.58	-3	-1.25	-2.18	1.83
Expected Total Return	2.52	2.96	-1.04	1.65	3.37	1.35	2.31	-1.11	-1.53	0.22	-0.71	3.3

*Excess and total returns are adjusted for the probability of occurrence. Adjusting Hong Kong for the impact of Tienamen Square in May and June, 1989, average annual returns for May and June would be 1.19 and 1.71 percent higher, respectively.

Data Source: Morgan Stanley Capital International.

Exhibit 8.10 Investment Strategies Suggested by Past Seasonal Patterns.

	Monthly Avg. Capital Appreciation	Long/Overweight			Short/Underweight		
		Open	Close	Expected Excess Return*	Open	Close	Expected Excess Return*
Japan	0.64%	Dec	Jan	2.1%	Sept	Nov	−4.1%
Hong Kong	2.14%	Dec	Feb	2.6%	Aug	Nov	−5.9%
Malaysia	1.68%	Oct	Feb	8.3%	Aug	Sept	−2.1%
Singapore	1.47%	Dec	Feb	4.4%	Aug	Nov	−8.7%

*Excess and total returns are adjusted by the probability of occurrence, and they refer only to capital returns, not to total returns.

SBC Warburg conducted a similar analysis of global equity market seasonality going back to 1975 for most of the major markets (Exhibit 8.11). The analysis shows patterns similar to the shorter time frame covered in this chapter. The methodology employed by SBC Warburg was as follows (Exhibit 8.12):

"Taking monthly market data back to 1975, extraordinary seasonal returns were calculated by taking the geometric mean of the difference between the monthly return and the annual return (converted back to show the typical monthly return over the whole year). Thus the tabulated values represent the average additional return from investing in that month whilst hedged against the return from the index over the year."[2]

[2] SBC Warburg, International Asset Briefing, August 11, 1995.

Exhibit 8.11 Seasonality in Global Equity Markets—Excess Returns (Confidence Levels), 1986–1995.

	Jan	Feb	Mar	Apr	May	June	July	Aug	Sep	Oct	Nov	Dec	Average Monthly Return*
Australia	0.27 (83)	-0.46 (82)	1.19 (10)	2.26 (72)	1.54 (11)	-2.21 (85)	3.33 (59)	0.60 (32)	-1.81 (59)	-3.85 (89)	-2.80 (85)	2.23 (48)	1.19
Canada	0.25 (75)	1.23 (20)	1.12 (25)	-1.02 (50)	1.40 (39)	-0.68 (48)	1.13 (6)	-0.39 (41)	-2.67 (91)	-1.24 (90)	-1.29 (39)	2.26 (68)	0.67
Denmark	3.77 (100)	-0.80 (97)	-1.31 (99)	0.17 (88)	2.15 (89)	0.81 (80)	0.57 (84)	-3.26 (99)	-2.45 (99)	0.30 (90)	-0.62 (99)	0.86 (84)	0.74
Finland	4.44 (90)	1.61 (50)	0.37 (67)	2.41 (38)	0.72 (62)	-2.22 (87)	2.86 (30)	-3.23 (91)	-5.64 (97)	2.54 (35)	0.26 (68)	-3.60 (93)	0.77
France	-0.41 (75)	4.27 (53)	1.77 (25)	2.52 (55)	-0.73 (56)	-2.95 (85)	1.67 (17)	-0.13 (41)	-3.54 (60)	-1.66 (69)	-1.18 (33)	0.65 (7)	0.95
Germany	-1.55 (2)	2.16 (63)	0.57 (58)	0.91 (64)	-0.51 (18)	0.56 (59)	1.47 (45)	0.54 (42)	-4.16 (34)	-0.98 (6)	-0.71 (24)	1.86 (77)	0.52
Hong Kong	-0.38 (98)	3.68 (64)	-2.25 (97)	0.55 (46)	2.86 (57)	-3.15 (84)	2.96 (51)	-3.05 (90)	-0.17 (97)	0.31 (60)	-3.49 (94)	2.50 (24)	2.14
Italy	2.11 (100)	2.66 (69)	2.98 (90)	3.79 (91)	-1.91 (98)	-2.48 (99)	1.65 (88)	-1.25 (75)	-4.29 (99)	-1.14 (99)	-3.63 (99)	1.93 (91)	0.74
Japan	1.54 (90)	-0.14 (66)	0.44 (25)	1.89 (0)	0.88 (63)	-4.11 (90)	2.32 (51)	0.92 (9)	-2.39 (88)	-0.85 (75)	-1.79 (82)	1.50 (49)	0.64

Malaysia	-2.33 (20)	3.37 (86)	-2.45 (3)	1.36 (68)	1.55 (70)	-0.85 (32)	0.97 (63)	-4.39 (43)	-1.44 (19)	1.96 (75)	-2.07 (6)	4.71 (93)	1.68
Netherlands	0.34 (99)	0.00 (93)	2.75 (3)	0.82 (39)	0.57 (95)	-0.07 (78)	1.58 (73)	-0.68 (82)	-2.56 (99)	-2.44 (96)	-1.70 (89)	1.53 (68)	1.03
Norway	3.08 (99)	1.13 (93)	2.40 (95)	0.69 (44)	1.49 (74)	-1.96 (96)	2.26 (46)	-0.61 (84)	-3.19 (95)	-4.52 (97)	-2.98 (96)	2.58 (87)	0.91
Singapore	1.07 (99)	1.92 (78)	-2.55 (98)	0.94 (19)	3.36 (57)	-0.15 (84)	0.91 (93)	-2.70 (96)	-3.07 (98)	-1.35 (92)	-2.28 (96)	4.23 (43)	1.47
Spain	3.76 (95)	1.60 (18)	0.51 (41)	0.86 (52)	2.58 (6)	-2.16 (80)	0.26 (76)	0.85 (66)	-4.25 (98)	-3.19 (93)	-0.34 (74)	-0.18 (81)	1.32
Sweden	2.39 (99)	2.23 (43)	0.77 (79)	1.49 (73)	3.07 (83)	-1.23 (95)	2.49 (30)	-3.14 (99)	-4.27 (99)	-2.34 (93)	-1.95 (76)	0.82 (70)	1.55
Switzerland	-0.17 (86)	0.39 (62)	0.27 (61)	-0.67 (51)	2.10 (47)	0.93 (7)	-0.03 (41)	-0.14 (26)	-1.96 (91)	-0.95 (46)	-0.93 (18)	1.23 (58)	0.90
United Kingdom	2.03 (99)	0.97 (84)	-0.23 (73)	0.32 (49)	0.62 (96)	-0.68 (93)	0.66 (88)	-0.71 (64)	-1.80 (97)	-2.40 (98)	-0.93 (77)	2.27 (55)	1.25
USA	1.73 (97)	1.20 (80)	-0.18 (67)	-0.47 (43)	1.98 (52)	-0.81 (58)	1.13 (47)	-0.44 (40)	-2.28 (95)	-2.11 (93)	-1.18 (33)	1.55 (21)	1.16

*Geometric Average

Data Source: Morgan Stanley Capital International Price Indices.

Exhibit 8.12 Extraordinary Seasonal Returns.

	Jan	Feb	Mar	Apr	May	Jun	Jul	Aug	Sep	Oct	Nov	Dec	Ave	Start Date*
Mexico-IPC Index	-0.70	-1.85	3.48	-0.34	7.20	-6.61	2.33	-2.47	-5.50	2.91	-0.80	0.03	54.03	Jan-88
Thailand-Set	1.70	-0.26	-0.17	0.39	0.53	2.20	1.47	-3.22	-2.52	-3.22	-5.83	4.80	31.81	Jan-86
Taiwan-Twsi	7.37	7.03	-0.58	4.50	-1.96	-7.59	4.25	-0.25	0.31	-10.69	2.45	-3.36	26.69	Jan-86
Hong Kong-Hang Seng	4.46	0.07	-3.68	2.02	0.07	-0.61	1.66	-1.56	-4.07	0.03	-2.64	2.86	19.90	
South Africa-JSE Overall	-0.01	-0.24	3.33	0.46	1.26	0.76	1.92	-3.24	-2.87	-0.30	-3.72	1.41	16.02	Apr-85
Sweden-VA Index	3.33	1.46	0.44	0.11	-0.59	-1.58	2.24	-2.41	-3.58	-1.03	-0.08	1.36	15.62	
Korea-Kopsi	-1.03	-0.68	1.41	-1.00	0.48	-0.05	0.70	-1.97	-0.93	-0.13	1.83	1.18	13.97	
UK-FT All Share	2.86	0.13	0.44	1.22	-1.63	-0.87	-0.55	0.81	-1.96	-2.66	-0.14	1.49	13.73	
Norway-OSLO SE	4.37	0.88	-0.52	2.23	0.81	-2.95	2.51	0.41	-1.67	-2.93	-3.58	1.41	13.71	
UK-FTSE100	2.42	0.46	0.14	1.35	-1.63	-0.68	-0.37	1.12	-2.15	-1.72	0.15	0.68	12.55	Jan-78
Finland-HEX General	2.73	1.29	1.42	0.68	0.50	-2.48	1.16	-1.08	-2.27	-0.40	-0.63	-0.81	11.64	
Australia-All Ordinaries	0.94	-2.11	0.10	2.04	1.09	-2.16	2.23	1.48	-0.82	-3.35	-2.27	1.57	11.58	
Italy-BCI Index	4.39	2.89	0.60	0.22	-1.17	-2.57	0.52	2.34	-2.85	-2.30	-2.05	0.04	11.27	
France-SBF 250	0.72	1.46	-0.46	2.82	-1.10	-2.22	0.18	1.12	-0.04	-2.72	-1.55	1.24	10.68	
New Zealand-NZSE40 Index	1.14	-0.22	-1.15	1.35	1.07	-0.13	1.17	1.65	-0.94	-0.75	-1.94	-1.85	10.26	
Netherlands-CBS All Share	2.16	-0.94	2.29	1.14	-1.51	0.20	0.26	-0.19	-2.54	-0.16	-0.50	0.77	9.73	

													Jan-80
Malaysia-KLSE Comp	0.47	2.16	-2.14	2.90	1.61	0.48	-1.67	-4.42	-1.07	-1.89	-2.41	3.77	9.59
Singapore DBS50	4.60	0.54	-1.78	2.43	1.32	0.43	-0.34	-2.24	-3.05	-2.15	-1.69	1.55	9.52
Denmark-Copenhagen SE	2.51	-0.83	0.13	0.40	0.00	0.63	0.71	-0.95	-2.36	-0.44	-1.69	1.05	9.17
US-S&P500	1.12	-0.63	-0.12	0.44	0.15	0.14	0.41	0.42	-1.90	-1.70	0.46	1.03	9.16
Japan-TOPIX	2.02	0.20	0.63	0.85	0.23	-1.21	-0.65	0.64	-2.02	-0.95	-1.65	1.68	8.98
Canada-TSE300	0.53	0.53	-0.24	-0.42	0.86	-0.56	0.47	1.10	-2.47	-2.52	0.98	1.95	7.82
Belgium-Brussels SE	1.71	2.15	0.48	0.63	-1.44	-1.35	0.49	-0.40	-1.10	-1.29	-1.52	1.46	7.08
Germany-FAZ	-0.39	0.56	1.10	0.56	-1.39	0.55	-0.07	-0.01	-1.59	-0.71	-0.37	1.14	7.08
Austria-Credit Aktien	-0.09	2.81	0.06	0.84	-0.23	-0.96	0.00	-0.24	-1.83	-1.85	-0.32	1.52	7.06
Switzerland-SBC General	1.13	-0.71	-0.25	-0.44	-0.50	0.69	0.12	0.35	-2.09	-0.83	0.05	1.88	6.99
Spain-Madrid SE	3.36	1.81	0.35	0.70	1.53	-0.83	0.41	-0.31	-3.44	-2.41	-0.85	-0.80	5.33

*Data were used from Jan. 1975, where available.

Data Source: SBC Warburg, International Asset Briefing, August 11, 1995.

9 The Bond Market and the Business Cycle

Bond market returns are a function of coupon income received from the bonds held; the capital gains or losses on the bonds in a portfolio and the level or rate at which coupon income received over the holding period can be reinvested. Aside from the risk of default, coupon income is known with certainty over the life of a bond or any given holding period. The certainty of coupon income, combined with its importance in overall bond returns, explains the low level of bond return volatility relative to other assets. Given the certainty surrounding coupon income flows, the crux of the decision on whether to hold bonds centers on expected capital gains or losses resulting from changes in market yields and coupon reinvestment risk. In the short to medium term, changes in market yields are determined by the progression of the business cycle.

Four factors dominate the determination of yield levels within the bond market. The most important factor is clearly expectations about inflation over the life of any given note or bond. These expectations determine the inflation premium embedded in fixed-income instruments.[1] The second factor is the real risk-free return to capital. The risk-free return is uniform across the maturity spectrum but not uniform across the time compendium. The risk-free rate of return is influenced by the global demand and supply of credit, and, at the margin, the aggregate

---

[1] There is clear econometric evidence to suggest that past inflationary experience heavily influences inflationary expectations and the inflation premia embedded in bond yields. Regression equations using 2-year trailing inflation (CPI) and 1-year forward inflation result in a significantly better fit than using forward inflation in isolation. The coefficients suggest a .65 weight for 24-month trailing inflation and a .26 weight for forward inflation.

level of government debt.[2] A third factor is the volatility of interest rates across the maturity spectrum.[3] Finally, country-specific structural factors, such as levels of government debt and current account balances, influence real rates of return via a sovereign risk premia for the bonds of different countries. At the subcountry level, corporate and municipal bonds have individual risk premia imparted to them via the market's perception of their specific risk.

BOND MARKET RETURNS AND THE GROWTH CYCLE

Bond market returns are less dependent on the phase and trajectory of the business cycle than on the stance of monetary policy. Returns to U.S. government bonds over the 18-year period from 1978 to 1995, under different economic and monetary conditions are presented in Exhibit 9.1. Over the 18-year period, the compound annual return for holding a U.S. government bond portfolio was 11.0 percent. Excess returns—returns above cash returns—were 5.0 percent.

Unequivocally, the direction of short-term interest rates dominates bond market performance regardless of the phase of the business cycle. However, the phase of the growth cycle often determines the trend in short-term rates and thus influences the bond market. There are, however, circumstances where unique factors or factors exogenous to the dynamics of the business cycle exert a dominant influence on monetary policy and short-term interest rates. For example, the oil price shocks of 1973 and 1979 resulted in extreme inflationary pressure within the economy, prompting aggressive Fed tightening. These two episodes resulted in policy-induced recessions, where monetary policy was out of

---

[2] The risk-free return to capital or the risk-free premia can be measured by netting the yield on short-term (30-day) default-free U.S. Treasury Bills minus contemporaneous inflation. Historically, the real risk-free rate averaged 1.4 percent from January 1972 to January 1994 and has fluctuated considerably, depending on the global demand and supply of capital and the stance of Fed policy. For the period from February 1974 to September 1979, the risk-free return was −1.62. The rate then jumped up to 3.46 on average from October 1979 to January 1987. From February 1987 to February 1994, the real risk-free return to capital averaged 1.7 percent.

[3] Volatility is measured by the standard deviation of rates through time. Interest rate volatility is influenced by the business cycle.

Exhibit 9.1 Bond Market Returns, the Growth Cycle and Monetary Policy, January 1978 to December 1995 (Standard Deviation of Returns in Parentheses).

	Phase I	Phase II	Phase III	Phase IV
	Negative & Decreasing (Narrowing) Output Gap	Positive & Increasing (Widening) Output Gap	Positive & Decreasing (Narrowing) Output Gap	Negative & Increasing (Widening) Output Gap
Increasing Short-Term Interest Rates				
Total Return	−3.5%	3.5%	−3.0%	−3.4%
Standard Deviation	(1.1%)	(1.4%)	(1.9%)	(2.1%)
Excess Return	−10.1%	−4.0%	−11.7%	−12.7%
Standard Deviation	(1.2%)	(1.4%)	(2.1%)	(2.2%)
Monthly Observations	20	51	27	10
Decreasing Short-Term Interest Rates				
Total Return	14.5%	22.6%	19.7%	27.8%
Standard Deviation	(1.3)	(1.6%)	(2.1%)	(1.7%)
Excess Return	8.3%	13.9%	10.6%	19.7%
Standard Deviation	(1.3%)	(1.65%)	(2.2%)	(1.5%)
Monthly Observations	19	28	32	29

Methodology: Quarterly total returns for each period of the growth cycle were chain-linked to compute an annualized geometric return for each phase. This approach permits reasonable comparison across various economic environments. Excess returns are returns above 3-month Treasury bills. Ninety-day Treasury bill yields were used for the measure of short-term interest rates. The standard deviation of total returns was computed using the log of returns to generate a log normal distribution. An increasing output gap is a gap that is moving further away from potential; a decreasing output gap is a gap that is moving in the direction of potential. Total return numbers are based on the Merrill Lynch total return index for U.S. government securities (all maturities).

sync with the growth dynamics of the economy because monetary policy was dictated by exogenously induced inflation.

The dominance of monetary policy—embodied in changes in short-term interest rates—is clearly apparent from Exhibit 9.1. The bottom panel, which represents months during which short-term interest rates were declining under all economic conditions, shows that bonds performed exceptionally well when short-term rates were falling, regardless of the phase of the business cycle. The top panel, which depicts monthly returns for all phases of the growth cycle when rates were rising, shows how poorly bonds did during these periods.

Negative Output Gaps and Bond Market Returns

Recessions are unambiguously good for bonds. In the short recession of 1980, bonds registered a 7.0 percent total return; the protracted recession of 1981–1982 resulted in a total return on U.S. Treasury bonds of 35.4 percent; and in the short recession of 1990–1991, bonds returned 11.7 percent.

The strongest performance registered by bonds has come when the output gap has been negative and deteriorating (Phase IV). During the period from January 1978 to December 1995, total annualized bond market returns during the 39 months when this situation prevailed were 18.95 percent. During periods when the economy was operating below potential and deteriorating and short-term interest rates were also declining, very impressive compound annual returns of 27.8 percent were registered. During this phase, deterioration in growth tended to prompt a decline in short-term interest rates as the Fed relaxed policy in an attempt to revive the economy. Of the 29 months during which the output gap was negative and deteriorating, 21 of those months occurred during or following the 1981–1982 or 1990–1991 recessions. During the recession of 1990–1991 and on into 1992, the Federal Reserve cut rates 23 times in an effort to stimulate growth.

In 9 of the 10 months when the economy was operating below potential and deteriorating, the Fed orchestrated a rise in short-term rates in an attempt to deal with the inflation triggered by the second oil price shock of 1979. Three of these occurrences followed the 1980 recession when the accommodative stance adopted during the recession was reversed immediately following the end of the recession, even though the output gap was widening. Six of the 10 instances occurred during the 1981–1982 recession when the Fed attempted to negotiate an orderly decline in interest rates in tandem with sharply falling inflation, but suffered periodic monthly reversals.

To the extent history is a guide, absent exogenous shocks, bonds can be expected to perform exceptionally well during periods of sharp deterioration in the economy.

During periods when the economy is performing below potential but improving, the direction of monetary policy has been split 50/50;

short-term interest rates increased in 20 out of 39 months. This is clearly due to the fact that a decreasing output gap implies an inflection point in the growth cycle. Inflection points are treacherous, as evidenced by the performance of bonds during these periods. To the extent the Fed believed the turn was assured, a reversal of monetary policy was normally warranted which, by definition, meant an increase in short-term interest rates. Historically, when a closing output gap was accompanied by rising short-term interest rates, bonds returned −3.5 percent per annum and an excess return of −10.1 percent per annum. If, however, the resumption of growth appeared tenuous and an accommodative monetary stance was maintained, bonds returned 14.5 percent per annum.

Positive Output Gaps and Bond Market Returns

The potentially negative impact of a positive output gap on the bond market has, in the past, often been offset by declining short-term interest rates (60 out of 138 months, or 43 percent of the time) to produce double-digit bond returns. The secular decline in interest rates in the early and mid-eighties explains most of the bond market returns during this period, even in periods when the economy was operating above a sustainable, noninflationary level. In large measure, the secular decline in inflation was attributable to the vigilance and increased credibility the Fed garnered in its tenacious efforts to wring inflation from the system.

Excess growth—growth above the level of noninflationary potential—generally triggers tighter monetary policy and rising short-term interest rates, which are negative for the bond market. The compound annual average total return to U.S. Treasury bonds during periods between January 1978 and December 1995 when growth has been above the sustainable trend has been 9.4 percent, with excess returns a scant 1.1 percent. Forty-three percent of the time, short-term interest rates were declining, even though growth was above trend. These rate declines generally occurred during months when the deviations of growth above potential were modest (less than 1 percent), or when the output gap was converging back to trend after having peaked. Ten of the 27 monthly episodes when the output gap was positive and decreasing but short-term interest rates were increasing occurred in response to the post-oil price shock of 1979.

During the 78 months, between January 1978 and December 1995, when growth was above potential and short-term interest rates were increasing, bonds did little more than mark time on a total return basis, and yielded negative excess returns after adjusting for cash returns. During the 60 months when the economy was operating above potential but experiencing declines in short-term interest rates, annualized bond market returns averaged between 22.6 percent and 19.7 percent, respectively, depending on whether the output gap was increasing or decreasing. Excess returns were 13.9 and 10.6 percent, respectively, over the same periods.

The dominant factor in determining bond market returns is the stance of monetary policy in response to either the business cycle or exogenous shocks to the system. In this light, the slavish focus of the bond market on the Federal Reserve is justified. Nevertheless, the economic cycle clearly shapes the environment the Fed monitors when setting monetary policy and short-term interest rates.

TRANSMISSION OF MONETARY IMPULSES

Assessment of the impact of monetary policy on financial markets requires an understanding and appreciation of the way in which monetary policy—particularly interest rate policy—affects the real economy and the fundamentals that underpin financial markets. Ironically, many of the structural changes that occurred in the U.S. economy over the past two decades have narrowed the focus of policy to changes in short-term interest rates, thereby simplifying the analysis.

The structural changes that occurred during the seventies and eighties have relegated the monetary aggregates—at one time, the all-important measures of the tone of monetary policy—to a tertiary consideration at best. The removal of the deposit rate ceiling; the introduction of NOW and money market accounts; the introduction of adjustable rate mortgages and mortgage-backed securities; and the floating of the dollar in the early seventies—all contributed to the breakdown in the relationship between

Exhibit 9.2　　U.S. Fed Funds Rate.

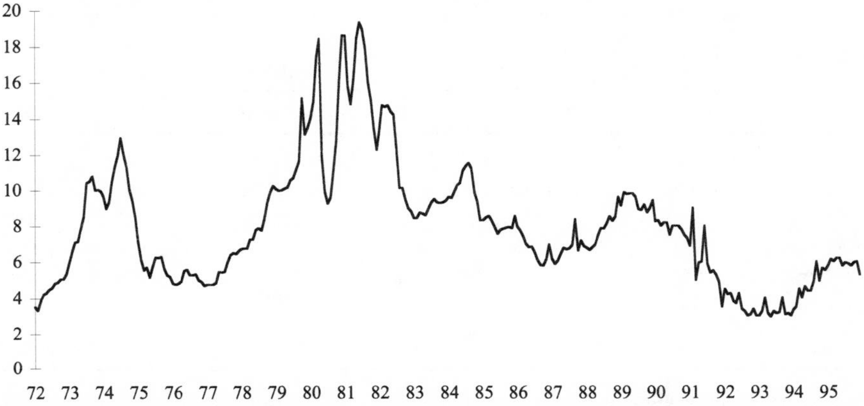

Data Source: Federal Reserve Board.

the monetary aggregates, the real economy, and interest rates. The focus of the Federal Reserve is now clearly on the trajectory of the economy and the appropriate level of interest rates.

The key transmission channels for monetary policy are via the cost of capital, the wealth effect and the exchange rate. An exploration of the key transmission mechanisms of interest rate policy, conducted by Eileen Mauskopf of the Board of Governors of the Federal Reserve, reveals that changes in the cost of capital and its impact on business fixed investment and residential construction are the most important channel for monetary impulses. The wealth effect and its impact on consumption is a close second. Changes in the exchange rate and its impact on net exports are a distant third (see Exhibit 9.3).[4]

Looking specifically at the sectors of the economy that are affected by changes in monetary policy reveals that changes in the cost of capital affect residential construction very quickly, within 4 quarters, while the

[4] Eileen Mauskopf, "The Transmission Channels of Monetary Policy: How Have They Changed?" *Federal Reserve Bulletin,* (December 1990), pp. 986–1008. Ms. Mauskopf provides an excellent overview of the transmission channels of monetary policy and its impact on the real economy. Much of the analysis looks at the impact of changes in interest rates on specific areas of the economy when allowing multiplier-accelerator interactions or feedbacks from goods markets to financial markets or prices.

Exhibit 9.3 Transmission Channels of Monetary Policy (Impact of a One Percentage Point Reduction in the Fed Funds Rate).

Quarters after Reduction	Cost of Capital			Wealth	Exchange Rate	Total
	Investment	Consumption	Total	Consumption	Net Exports	Total
			Percent of Total Effect			
4 Qtrs	50%	18%	68%	14%	18%	100%
8 Qtrs	45%	5%	50%	22%	28%	100%
12 Qtrs	45%	1%	46%	31%	24%	100%
16 Qtrs	55%	1%	56%	33%	12%	100%
20 Qtrs	55%	*	55%	41%	4%	100%
Average			55%	28%	17%	100%

*Less than 0.5 percent.

Data Source: Eileen Mauskopf, "The Transmission Channels of Monetary Policy: How Have They Changed?" *Federal Reserve Bulletin* (December 1990), p. 987. The exhibit reflects the effects on spending of a reduction of 1 percentage point in the federal funds rate, by transmission channel. The estimates are generated using the Federal Reserve's MPS econometric model of the U.S. economy.

impact on business fixed investment is initially muted, but ultimately has a significant impact after 12 to 16 quarters (see Exhibit 9.4). The short lag time between changes in interest rates and changes in residential construction reflects the substantial impact of changes in interest rates on the monthly payments and affordability of residential ownership. The delayed impact on business investment clearly reflects the long decision time required for changes in corporate investment plans.

It is interesting to note that the impact on consumption is primarily via the wealth effect and not through consumer debt servicing[5] (see Exhibit 9.3). The impact on consumption via the wealth effect is substantial, culminating in 41 percent of the total impact of a change in policy rates 20 quarters out.

[5] Interest rate changes affect consumer wealth in several ways. Increasing short-term interest rates translate into higher rates on short-term money market instruments, with a lag, and thus benefit holders of these instruments. Rising rates, however, generally adversely impact the capital value of both bonds and equities and thus result in a decline in wealth. Lower rates have the opposite effect, benefiting holders of long maturity investment instruments such as stocks and bonds while hurting holders of short term money market instruments.

Exhibit 9.4 Transmission Channels of Monetary Policy (Impact of a 1 Percentage Point Reduction in the Fed Funds Rate).

Quarters after Reduction	Investment					
	Residential Construction	Business Fixed	Inventory	Consumption	Net Exports	Total
	Percent of Total Effect					
4 Qtrs	33%	7%	10%	32%	18%	100%
8 Qtrs	25%	13%	7%	26%	28%	100%
12 Qtrs	22%	20%	3%	32%	24%	100%
16 Qtrs	25%	28%	2%	34%	12%	100%
20 Qtrs	21%	33%	1%	42%	4%	100%

Data Source: Eileen Mauskopf, "The Transmission Channels of Monetary Policy: How Have They Changed?", *Federal Reserve Bulletin* (December 1990), p. 987. The exhibit reflects the effects on spending of a reduction of 1 percentage point in the federal funds rate. The estimates are generated using the Federal Reserve's MPS econometric model of the U.S. economy.

The impact on net exports emerges as fairly substantial some 4 to 8 quarters after the change in interest rates, and it peaks at 28 percent of the total impact of a change in interest rates[6] (Exhibit 9.4).

The lag structure of changes in interest rates and their impact on the real economy are critical for an assessment of the appropriate stance of monetary policy. The work done by E. Mauskopf indicates that 24 percent of the impact of a change in interest rates will be realized within 4 quarters; 44 percent, within 8 quarters and 69 percent, within 12 quarters. Residential construction and consumption respond the most to interest rate changes in the short term. A contemporaneous reading of the economy and interest rates can clearly convey false signals if earlier interest rate changes are not explicitly considered. An assessment of the source of growth or weakness (e.g., weak consumer spending) is also important, given the disparate impact on sectors for a given change in rates.

[6] Changes in interest rates often have a significant impact on exchange rates and thus impact net exports.

THE TAYLOR RULE, FED POLICY AND THE FEDERAL FUNDS RATE

Under the Federal Reserve Act, the Fed has the task of maintaining "stable prices" and "maximum employment."[7] The key policy variable the Fed has employed in recent years to achieve these two goals—following the breakdown of the monetary aggregates—is the level of the federal funds rate. Given the impact of monetary policy on asset prices, forecasting or predicting changes in the federal funds rate is one of the most important exercises an investor undertakes.

Professor John Taylor of Stanford University has suggested a "policy rule" for monetary policy. The rule provides an equation that implies an appropriate "neutral" rate for the federal funds rate, given changes in the price level or changes in overall economic activity.[8] The "Taylor Rule" has, in fact, been quite accurate in predicting where the Federal Reserve Open Market Committee (FOMC) would set the federal funds rate over the past decade (see Exhibit 9.5). The rule suggested by Taylor's work is as follows:

$$\text{Fed Funds Rate} = P + .5((QGDP - TGDP)/TGDP) + .5(P - 2.0) + 2$$

where

Fed Funds Rate = average for the quarter;

P   = GDP deflator for previous four quarters;

QGDP   = changes in quarterly real GDP annualized;

TGDP   = trend real GDP (often interpreted as potential GDP).

---

[7] Federal Reserve Act, 12 U.S.C. § 225, December 23, 1913.

[8] John B. Taylor, "Discretion Versus Policy Rules in Practice," Center for Economic Policy Research, Publication No. 327, November, 1992. Professor Taylor's work draws on and incorporates his own recent work and others' work on "rational expectations" models in macroeconomics and the importance of credibility, read, predictability in policy setting in a rational expectations framework.

Variations of the "Taylor Rule" can usefully be applied to other countries where monetary policy is implemented by the management of short-term policy interest rates.

Exhibit 9.5 Taylor Rule and the Federal Funds Rate.

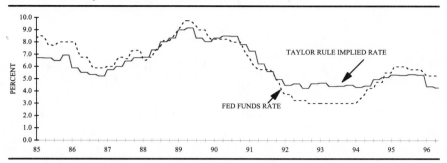

The implied Federal Reserve targets embedded in the Taylor Rule are:

Inflation target of 2.0 percent

Real fed funds target of 2.0 percent.

(The target levels embedded in the formula can be changed as appropriate.)

The salient features of the rule are that the fed funds rate would rise if inflation increased above a target of 2.0 percent or if real GDP rose above trend or potential GDP. Conversely, if inflation or GDP growth falls below target or trend respectively, the Fed would reduce the federal funds rate in response. If growth and inflation are on target, then the neutral fed funds rate would be 4.0 percent in nominal terms and 2.0 percent in real terms. In theory, the real rate should be close to the long-term trend/real growth rate of the economy.[9] By focusing on the output gap and inflation, the Taylor Rule has embedded in it the Phillips curve inflation/unemployment trade-off and the Fed's twin goals of stable prices and maximum employment.

The focus of Taylor's work is not on forecasting the federal funds rate, but on providing financial markets and economic participants with a methodology for understanding likely Fed responses to disequilibria in the economic system. "Rational expectations" theory contends that informed market participants and economic participants

[9] Alison Stuart, "Simple Monetary Policy Rules," *Bank of England Quarterly Bulletin,* August 1996, pp. 282–287.

Exhibit 9.6   U.S. Output Gap and Inflation.

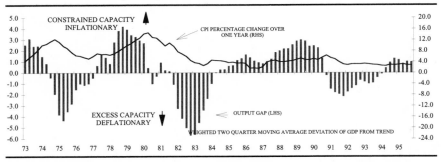

Data Source: GDP—Bureau of Economic Analysis; CPI—Bureau of Labor Statistics.

will react "rationally" to expected changes in monetary policy, thereby reducing the required magnitude of swings within the system because participants can be "assured" that appropriate policy action will be taken to correct any disequilibrium situation that might develop.

Investors will find the Taylor Rule useful in making judgments about the likely path of monetary policy at different stages of the business and growth cycle given its value in predicting monetary policy changes. Over the 11-year period from 1985 to 1996, the model has had an adjusted R^2 of .80. Over the period from 1973 to 1996, the R^2 was .40, which is low but understandable given the extensive level of credit controls in the seventies and early eighties, which would have reduced the relevance of the federal funds rate.

The Taylor Rule is even more valuable when one considers that, over the 24-year period from February 1972 to February 1996, long-term interest rates declined in only 43 months when short-term rates were rising. More importantly, long-term rates fell significantly (more than 25 basis points) in only 12 of these months—and most of these falls occurred under unusual circumstances (see Exhibit 9.7). Conversely, both short- and long-term rates moved in tandem during 245 months out of the 288 months, or 85 percent of the time. The large declines in long-term rates when short-term rates increased were precipitated by substantial, credible increases in short-term rates that would clearly slow the economy and, in doing so, dampen inflation.

Exhibit 9.7   Opposite Moves in 90-Day Treasury Bill Yields and 10-Year Treasury Bond Yields.

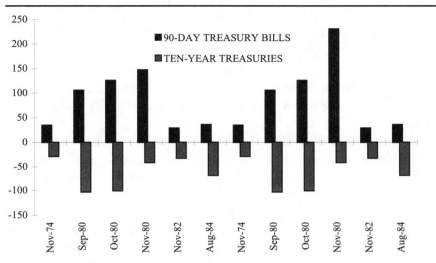

Given this history, the insights available from the application of the Taylor Rule are quite significant.

In the fall of 1974, in response to the double-digit inflation induced by the oil shock of 1972–1973 and excessive demand in the economy, the Fed pushed up short-term interest rates and caused an inverted yield curve (which is almost always a precursor to recession), thereby breaking inflationary expectations and resulting in falling long-term yields. The second oil shock, in 1979, again sent inflation soaring and prompted the Fed, under the direction of Chairman Paul Volker, to push up the federal funds rate sharply, again causing an inverted yield curve thereby nullifying any tendency to validate inflation within the economy.

THE GROWTH CYCLE, THE NAPM INDEX AND THE FEDERAL FUNDS RATE

The National Association of Purchasing Managers (NAPM) Index is one of the most widely followed and timely economic indicators monitored by financial market participants. The NAPM Index is compiled from the responses of over 300 major purchasing managers regarding new orders, production, employment, delivery times and inventories. The Index is a diffusion index. Index levels above 50 imply expanding activity in the manufacturing sector and readings below 50 imply contraction. Typically, readings below 45 are associated with recessions. The Index is an exceedingly good indicator of the performance of the economy, as is evident by the strong correlation between the NAPM Index and year-on-year GDP growth (see Exhibit 9.8).

Because the NAPM Index is such an important leading indicator of the performance of the economy, it is also valuable as a guide to changes in monetary policy. The scatter diagram (Exhibit 9.9) sets out the relationship between NAPM Index levels over the past 13½ years and changes in the federal funds rate. What is clear is that index levels above 55 are generally a good indication that the economy is on an expansionary path that is unsustainable without inflationary pressure and that monetary policy will have a contractionary or tightening bias. That is, 86 percent of the changes in the federal funds rate when the NAPM Index was above 55 were for higher rather than lower interest rates. Conversely, when the NAPM Index was below 45, the policy bias was reversed. In the range between 45 and 55, the bias is marginally skewed toward rate declines.

Another key index worth monitoring is the NAPM deliveries index or vendor index, which appears to be a particular favorite of the Federal

Exhibit 9.8   NAPM Index Level and U.S. GDP Growth.

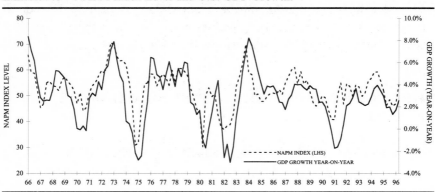

Exhibit 9.9 NAPM Index and Changes in the Federal Funds Rate (December 1982–June 1996).

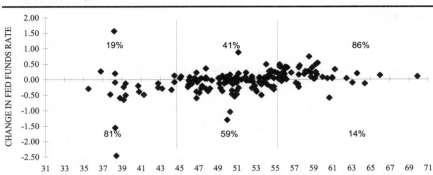

Reserve (Exhibit 9.10). The deliveries index is an early warning signal for increasing delivery times, a symptom of emerging capacity constraints within the manufacturing sector of the economy. As capacity constraints are associated with inflationary pressures, this index is an early warning sign of potential inflation and changes in monetary policy in response. As Exhibit 9.10 indicates, whenever the delivery index moves above 53, there is a very strong bias that the federal funds rate will increase. Over the 13½-year period covered in the exhibit, the federal funds rate increased 87 percent of the time when the NAPM delivery index was above 53.

Exhibit 9.10 NAPM Deliveries Index and Changes in the Federal Funds Rate (December 1982–June 1996).

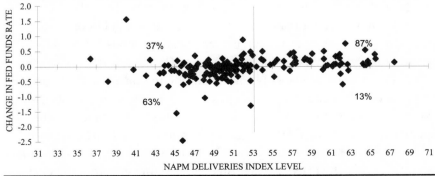

Below 53, the bias was reversed, albeit somewhat less pronounced with declines experienced 63 percent of the time when the index registered delivery levels below 53.

THE YIELD CURVE AND THE GROWTH CYCLE

The yield curve represents the yield to maturity for bills, notes and bonds of similar credit quality for all terms available (for the U.S. debt market, the yield curve represents terms from 3 months to 30 years). In general, references to the yield curve refer to the U.S. Treasury yield curve. Market participants often refer to the "coupon curve," which includes coupon-bearing notes and bonds and is normally measured by the spread between 2-year and 30-year Treasuries. The "bill curve" is also monitored to assess short-term policy expectations.

Embedded in the yield curve are explicit expectations about the future course of inflation, fixed-income market volatility, and monetary policy, all of which are influenced and, to a large extent, determined by the growth cycle of the economy. The yield curve contains a wealth of information about market expectations regarding the future course of economic fundamentals and the stance of monetary policy (Exhibit 9.11).

Characterizations of the yield curve and statements about the stance of monetary policy based on the shape of the curve can overgeneralize what is often a complicated picture of the interaction of economic fundamentals and monetary policy. Nevertheless, generalizations can be useful as a departure point for making assessments and decisions about bond market investments.

The yield curve benchmarks off current and expected inflation. (Current inflation has the greatest influence on short-term interest rates; expected inflation is relevant for longer-duration bonds.) The slope and shape of the yield curve—the steepness or flatness of the curve as well as the curvature—are heavily influenced by the business cycle and the trajectory of the economy. The slope of the yield curve measures the difference between long- and short-term interest rates and is generally specified in terms of 10-year Treasuries minus 3-month Treasury bills, or 30-year Treasuries minus 2 year Treasuries. The real risk-free return to capital—which varies through time but is uniform across the curve—

Exhibit 9.11   U.S. Output Gap and the Yield Curve.

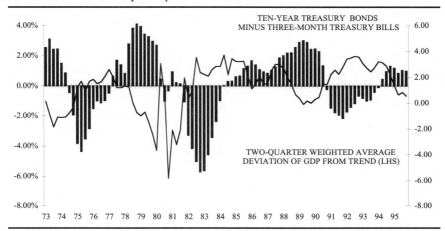

and the volatility or risk premium—which increases with maturity—also influence the level of the yield curve.[10]

The slope of the yield curve (Exhibit 9.12) is heavily influenced by the interaction of inflationary expectations and expectations about changes in monetary policy, both of which are driven by the business cycle.[11]

In general, a steep curve, where short-term rates are more than 275 basis points below long-term rates, is indicative of a very accommodative monetary policy stance where the Federal Reserve is specifically endeavoring to stimulate economic activity by setting the federal funds target rate low. A "steep curve" is often evident at the trough of the business cycle or in periods when the economy is operating below potential (see Exhibit 9.11).

[10] There is clear statistical evidence to suggest that the volatility of interest rates is influenced by the level of rates and that there is a "base" effect that causes higher interest rate environments generally to experience higher levels of volatility.

[11] Some analysts prefer to assess the yield curve using the ratio between long and short rates as opposed to the difference. The ratio approach probably has some advantages when there are quantum changes in the level of inflation and the inflation premia embedded in bond yields. Assuming a constant equilibrium ratio relationship implies, ceteris parabis, a steepening of the curve as the level of rates increases and a flattening of the curve as rates fall. This may, in fact, be a reasonable assumption if one assumes that bondholders require a higher risk premium for holding bonds in high inflationary environments and a lower risk premium in low inflationary environments.

Exhibit 9.12   Types of Yield Curves.

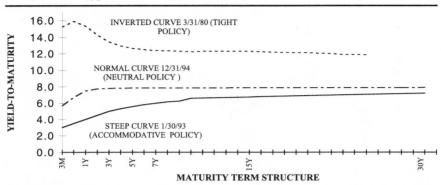

The existence of a steep yield curve can have very negative implications for bond market returns. The presence of a steep curve implies accommodative monetary policy designed to stimulate economic activity. To the extent the policy is successful, economic activity will improve, resulting in a reduction of excess capacity in the capital and labor markets and attendant upward pressure on prices. Acceleration of inflation will subsequently prompt a tightening of monetary policy and rising short-term interest rates. The bond investor will experience the worst of all worlds: Short-term rates will be rising as policy is tightened while inflationary expectations are simultaneously increasing. In short, unless the policy fails and an even more stimulative stance is adopted via a lower federal funds target rate, interest rates have only one way to go and that is up.

A "normal yield curve" can be characterized by a differential of between 150 to 250 basis points between short and long rates, with the mean centered on 200 basis points (Exhibit 9.13). From 1985 to 1995, the spread between short- and long-term rates averaged 200 basis points with a standard deviation of 109 basis points. This is significantly higher than the experience of the 24-year period from 1972 to early 1996, when the risk premium for the 10-year U.S. Treasury bonds averaged 130 basis points (Exhibit 9.14). Normal shaped yield curves are evident when the economy is progressing at trend growth or in line with

Exhibit 9.13 Yield Curve Frequency Distribution (1985–1995).

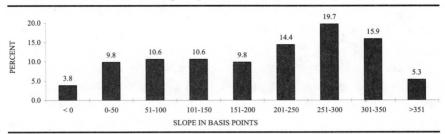

potential noninflationary growth. Monetary policy is generally neutral on these occasions.

A "flat yield curve" is generally present for a fairly limited period of time and is a transitional state between other yield curve structures. A flat curve is often present at inflection points in the growth cycle, where the economy is moving from a positive to a negative output gap or vice versa. At inflection points, the macroeconomic data can be inconclusive and contradictory and may present a mixed view of the economy, making an assessment of the direction of economic activity difficult.

"Yield curve inversions"—where short-term rates are higher than long-term rates—are induced by the Federal Reserve Open Market Committee and are in response to external inflationary shocks such as the oil price shocks of the seventies or inflationary overheating in the economy. "Inverted yield curves" are inevitably precursors to recession. This was certainly the case in 1979 and early 1980, when the inversion

Exhibit 9.14 Yield Curve Characteristics.*

	Jan 1985– Dec 1995	Jan 1983– Apr 1996	Jan 1972– Dec 1984	Jan 1972– Dec 1995
Mean	200	218	60	130
Median	226	242	109	162
Standard Deviation	109	100	194	174
Minimum	−31	5	−583	−583
Maximum	381	374	360	374

*Ten-year Treasuries minus 3-month Treasury bills.

culminated at −366 basis points at the end of March, precipitating the recession of 1980. Again in 1980–1981, in response to the oil price shock, the Fed pushed up the federal funds rate, causing a sharp, protracted inversion that precipitated the recession of 1981–1982. Inverted yield curves contain unambiguous policy signals from the Fed and should not be ignored. Historically, yield curve inversions have often been extreme in magnitude in terms of the slope of the curve and have, at times, continued for protracted periods of time (see Exhibit 9.15). Yield curve inversions are set at the short end of the curve and are orchestrated through the target level for the federal funds rate.

Curve inversions can have a favorable impact on bond returns if the high short-term rates are successful in wringing inflation out of the economy. Persistent, high short-term rates normally result in a slowing of economic growth and/or a contraction in the economy, with attendant declines in inflation and commensurate rallies in bonds. It can, however, be a delicate task to determine the level at which the inversion will be successful at curing inflation. The credibility of the Fed is critical when assessing a bond strategy during an inversion. Ceteris paribus, an inversion of any consequence for a measurable period of time should result in a sharp contraction of economic activity and a decline in inflationary expectations and bond yields.

Exhibit 9.15   U.S. Yield Curve.

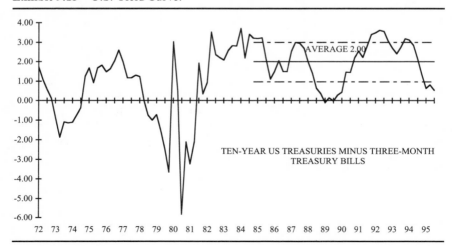

TEN-YEAR US TREASURIES MINUS THREE-MONTH
TREASURY BILLS

BOND MARKET RETURNS AND CHANGES IN THE LEVEL AND SHAPE OF THE YIELD CURVE

Aside from coupon income received from holding bonds, the most important factor in determining returns to a bond portfolio is changes in the level of interest rates. The second most important factor is changes in the slope of the yield curve, and, finally, changes in the curvature of the curve. A study by Litterman and Scheinkman empirically verified these somewhat obvious observations using regression analysis and zero-coupon Treasuries.[12] The results of their findings are summarized in Exhibit 9.16.[13]

The obvious conclusion from this research is that the most important consideration for a bond investor is the direction of interest rates, which, historically, accounted for 89.5 percent of the returns while shifts in the

Exhibit 9.16   Zero Coupon U.S. Treasury Returns.

Maturity	Total Explained Variance (R SQD)	Proportion of Explained Variance		
		Changes in Level of Interest Rates	Changes in Yield Curve Slope	Changes in Curvature of the Yield Curve
6 Months	99.5	79.5	17.2	3.2
1 Year	99.4	89.7	10.1	0.2
2 Years	98.2	93.4	2.4	4.2
5 Years	98.8	98.2	1.1	0.7
8 Years	98.7	95.4	4.6	0
10 Years	98.8	92.9	6.9	0.2
14 Years	98.4	86.2	11.5	2.2
18 Years	95.3	80.5	14.3	5.2
Average	98.4	89.5	8.5	2.0

Data Source: Robert Litterman and Jose Scheinkman, "Common Factors Affecting Bond Returns," *Journal of Fixed Income* (June 1991), p. 58.

[12] Robert Litterman and José Scheinkman, "Common Factors Affecting Bond Returns," *Journal of Fixed Income* (June 1991), p. 58.
[13] Similar results were derived in a study of yield curve shifts by Frank J. Jones, "Yield Curve Strategies," *Journal of Fixed Income* (September 1991), pp. 33–41. Jones's work covers the period from 1979 to 1990 and finds that 91.6 percent of the returns to Treasuries are attributable to parallel and twists in the yield curve.

slope and curvature of the yield curve accounted for only 10.5 percent
of the returns.

NOMINAL VERSUS REAL INTEREST RATES

Any evaluation of interest rates and bond market investment decisions
ultimately focuses on the issue of real versus nominal interest rates and
the "appropriate" real or inflation-adjusted rate. This is because bondholders are compensated in the form of an inflation premium, a risk-free
return to capital and a risk premium. Although a determination of the
appropriate inflation premium can be problematical, reasonable judgments can be made about the appropriate inflation premia using forward
consensus inflation estimates, or econometric models based on past experience. (See Chapter 10 for an analysis of comparative inflation premia across markets.)

The risk-free return to capital varies over time, in response to global
demand and supply considerations. The risk premium associated with
bonds can usefully be decomposed into a volatility premium and a sovereign risk premium.[14] The volatility premium can be estimated using
regression analysis to measure the return associated with different levels of volatility, and then observing contemporaneously implied volatility in the options market.

The sovereign risk premium is a function of country-specific factors
such as the level of government debt, the government deficit and the current account deficit. The credibility of monetary and fiscal policy also
factors into the level of the sovereign risk premium.

APPENDIX 9.1 TERM STRUCTURE OF
INTEREST RATES

The yield curve graphically depicts the relationship between the yield
on Treasury securities and maturity. The term structure of interest rates

---

[14] In the case of corporate bonds, the soverign risk premia would be replaced by a company
specific risk premia.

Exhibit 9.17   U.S. Real 10-Year Treasury Bond Yield.*

* Ten-year Treasuries minus CPI.

is derived from the U.S. Treasury yield curve and is a theoretical spot rate curve based on zero-coupon Treasury instruments and arbitrage relationships.[15] In essence, the term structure of interest rates consists of a strip of spot rates for discrete periods of time in the future. Forward rates are one-period future reinvestment rates implied by spot rates. Forward rates are derived by breaking down the spot rate curve into a set of discrete time periods that begin at a specified time in the future and end at an even later time in the future. Forward rates can also be viewed as market consensus rates of future spot rates.[16]

Three general theories attempt to explain the term structure of interest rates: (1) unbiased expectations; (2) liquidity preference and (3) the market segmentation theory.[17] A brief discussion of these theories provides a useful backdrop for considering the impact of the business cycle on interest rates.

The unbiased expectations theory asserts that the forward rate represents the general market view of the expected future spot rate for the

[15] *See* Frank J. Fabozzi, *Fixed Income Mathematics* (Chicago: Probus Publishing Co., 1993), chap. 13.
[16] Frank J. Fabozzi and Gifford Fong, *Advanced Fixed Income Portfolio Management* (Chicago: Probus Publishing Co., 1994) p. 22.
[17] A useful overview of these theories and a synopsis of the empirical work supporting the theories are presented in John H. Wood and Norma L. Wood, *Financial Markets* (New York: Harcourt Brace Jovanovich, 1985).

period in question. Further, the future spot rate will reflect a combination of inflationary expectations as well as an assessment of the real rate of return for the period in question. The expectations theory thus reflects expectations about future inflation, but also expectations about monetary policy (in the form of policy interest rates). Although the unbiased expectations theory provides useful insights, it does not explain the bias for the yield curve to be upward sloping over time. The liquidity preference theory sheds some light on the curve's upward sloping bias. The premise of the theory is that investors prefer short-term securities or liquidity to longer-dated securities, and investors must be paid a premium if they invest in longer-dated securities and sacrifice liquidity. This risk premium is represented by the difference between the forward rate and the expected future spot rate or the rate represented by the yield curve. The market segmentation theory holds that various investors and borrowers, or classes of investors and borrowers, have specific preferences and needs that dictate the maturity structure they favor. The demand and supply dictated by these preferences and circumstances determine the term structure of interest rates.

SELECTED REFERENCES

Blinder, Alan S. Remarks at the Senior Executives Conference of the Mortgage Bankers Association, New York, January 10, 1996.

Fabozzi, Frank J. *Fixed Income Mathematics.* Chicago: Probus Publishing Co., 1993.

Fabozzi, Frank J., and Fong, Gifford. *Advanced Fixed Income Portfolio Management.* Chicago: Probus Publishing Co., 1994.

Farrell, James L., Jr. *Guide to Portfolio Management.* New York: McGraw-Hill, 1983.

Federal Reserve Act, 12 USC § 226, December 23, 1913.

Jones, Frank J. "Yield Curve Strategies," *Journal of Fixed Income* (September 1991), pp. 33–41.

Litterman, Robert, and Scheinkman, José. "Common Factors Affecting Bond Returns." *Journal of Fixed Income* (June 1991), pp. 54–61.

Mauskopf, Eileen "The Transmission Channels of Monetary Policy: How Have They Changed?" *Federal Reserve Bulletin* (December 1990).

Sharpe, William F., and Alexander, Gordon J. *Investments,* Englewood Cliffs, NJ: Prentice-Hall, 1990.

Stuart, Alison. "Simple Monetary Policy Rules," *Bank of England Quarterly Bulletin* (August 1996), pp. 282–287.

Taylor, John B. "Discretion Versus Policy Rules in Practice." Center for Economic Policy, Research Publication No. 327, November 1992.

Wood, John H., and Wood, Norma L. *Financial Markets.* New York: Harcourt Brace Jovanovich, 1985.

10 Global Bond Markets

GLOBAL BOND MARKET INTEGRATION

Global bond markets are highly integrated with few impediments to the free flow of capital among the major markets of the world. The increased integration and openness of the global market have, in many instances, added to periodic bouts of extreme volatility as leveraged international players such as the major commercial and merchant banks and the so-called "hedge funds" aggressively move money from market to market.

An interesting example of the openness of markets and the freedom with which money is moved around the world in search of investment opportunities is provided by the widely followed strategy of some of the major hedge funds in early 1996. These funds were borrowing in the short-term yen money market at half a percent and converting the proceeds into U.S. dollars, then buying U.S. 30-year Treasury bond futures with only 2.7 percent posted as margin. These positions were leveraged up to 37 times, with the expectation that U.S. bonds would rally and the yen would depreciate, providing profits in U.S. dollars and repayment of the borrowed yen at a lower rate. With leverage like this, small adverse moves can be very negative and precipitate major shifts in positions in a compressed time frame. The "threshold of pain" for these market players is very low.

Global bond markets benchmark off the U.S. bond market. This is clearly evident from Exhibit 10.1, a correlation matrix that shows the world's major bond markets over the 10-year period from 1986 to 1995. The last column in the matrix presents the correlation of each of the major markets with the U.S. market. For example, the correlation

Exhibit 10.1 Salomon World Government Bond Index Correlation Matrix (1986–1995).

	AUS	CAN	FRA	GER	ITA	JAP	NET	SPA	UK	US
Australia	**6.3%**	32.5%	22.2%	24.6%	16.0%	13.1%	27.2%	23.7%	27.5%	31.7%
Canada		**6.5%**	41.9%	43.7%	20.0%	37.5%	41.0%	27.4%	51.5%	72.0%
France			**4.9%**	74.7%	63.5%	38.7%	75.9%	62.7%	58.2%	49.9%
Germany				**3.6%**	48.2%	51.8%	91.6%	49.2%	63.2%	49.3%
Italy					**5.2%**	10.9%	48.9%	68.0%	45.9%	21.1%
Japan						**4.9%**	44.6%	6.1%	44.2%	41.5%
Netherlands							**3.6%**	47.2%	59.6%	47.9%
Spain								**3.4%**	44.0%	6.1%
UK									**7.5%**	44.4%
US										**5.1%**

Volatility (standard deviation) in bold on the diagonal.

Data Source: BARRA World Markets Model. Monthly total return data from Salomon Brothers World Government Bond Index. In local market terms.

between the U.S. bond market and the Canadian bond market over the 10-year period was 72.0 percent. The core European markets had a correlation of around 50 percent with the U.S. bond market over the 10-year period.[1] European markets, particularly the core European markets, are also highly correlated with Germany; for example, Germany registered correlations of 74.7 and 91.6 percent against France and the Netherlands. Correlations between the major markets is even higher when comparisons are made using 10-year government bond yields. This is largely due to the differing maturity structure of the markets, which distorts the sensitivity of the markets to foreign interest rate changes. Correlations between U.S. 10-year Treasury bonds and 10-year government bonds of the Group of Seven (G7) countries, over the five years ended December 1995, were as follows: United Kingdom, .89 percent; Germany, .82 percent; France, .76 percent; Japan, .74 percent; Italy, .46 percent and Canada, .93 percent.

The degree of correlation of any given market at any given time is highly dependent on the degree of synchronization of that market's growth and inflation cycle with other major markets. The high degree of correlation within Europe is to be expected given the substantial level of integration of the European economies and the European Exchange Rate Mechanism. The lower correlations evident between Japan, Italy, Spain and Australia reflect the low degree of synchronization of these markets' growth cycles.

REAL VERSUS NOMINAL INTEREST RATES

Any discussion of global bond markets inevitably focuses on real interest rates because of the cross-country distortions caused by inflationary differentials among countries. In part, this is merely an analytic step intended to make the investment decision tractable, and in part, it

---

[1] To some degree, the low correlations between the U.S. and Japan and Australia are due to the fact that these markets are one day ahead of the U.S. market. The different time zone result in some distortion as the U.S. market is the dominant market. Lagging these markets by one day results in a higher correlation. Time zone differentials are less of a problem for the European markets because there is a time overlap with the U.S. market.

is because many market participants assume that, to a large extent, inflationary differentials among countries are offset, over time, by currency rate adjustments.

Standard economic theory suggests that real interest rates equate the desired level of savings with the planned level of investment. The decline in savings rates in the major industrial countries since the sixties combined with the increase in aggregate government debt levels over the same time period implies an increase in real interest rates. This is exactly what has happened. An extensive study of real interest rates, carried out by the Group of Ten (G-10) Deputies, bears this out. The study indicates that real long-term interest rates have increased about 100 basis points over the past 35 years, from around 3.0 percent to around 4.0 percent.[2] The study also indicates that the increases have been common to most G-10 countries.

The G-10 Deputies' work is corroborated by work done by the Research Department of the International Monetary Fund which indicates that real interest rates averaged 1 to 2 percent in the sixties and early seventies, dropped to zero during the oil shock period of 1973 to 1980, and then moved dramatically higher (3 to 4.5 percent) from 1981 to 1994. The International Monetary Fund (IMF) study attributes the increase to the increase in world government debt relative to GDP and the increase in the rate of return on productive capacity.[3]

According to the work done by the G-10 Deputies, since the sixties, gross national savings in the G-10 countries has declined five percentage points to under 20 percent of GDP. The major contributory factor is a rise in fiscal deficits. Over the same period, desired investment has moderated only modestly—hence, the inevitable upward adjustment in real interest rates. Additionally, although significant emphasis has been placed on the capital demands of emerging and transitional economies, the G-10 work indicated that the bulk of their capital was generated

[2] Group of Ten Deputies Report, "Savings, Investment and Real Interest Rates," October 1995. See also Nigel Jenkinson, "Savings, Investment and Real Interest Rates," *Bank of England Quarterly Bulletin* (February 1996) pp. 51–62, for an excellent summary of the extensive research conducted in support of the Group of Ten report.

[3] Thomas Helbling and Robert Wescott, "The Global Real Interest Rate," Staff Studies for the World Economic Outlook, International Monetary Fund.

from savings within these countries and has not been a significant factor affecting global capital markets.[4]

Global capital markets have become significantly more integrated as domestic credit allocation controls have been dismantled, along with the elimination of virtually all restrictions on capital mobility among markets.[5] The very high degree of capital mobility, combined with the minimal level of domestic capital market distortions, implies a single rate of return to capital in all markets after adjusting for domestic market risk and exchange rate distortions. That is, real interest rates are determined by global savings and investment and not by country-specific factors. The implications of a global, integrated capital market is that individual countries will, at times, be assessed very substantial risk premia when their policies are deemed unsound by financial markets.

Econometric work conducted by economists at the Bank of England indicates that the level of government debt as a proportion of GDP explained 28 to 43 percent of the level of real interest rates during the three periods of medium (1959–1973), low (1974–1979) and high (1980–1992) real interest rates. Current government consumption as a proportion of GDP was the next most important explanatory variable explaining 17 to 19 percent of the level of real rates. Changes in M1 were also important, lagged one and two periods explaining 15 to 18 percent (see Exhibit 10.2).

The study also found that changes in the average government debt–GDP ratio for the ten countries involved in the three interest rate regimes were extremely significant in explaining changes in the levels of both long- and short-term real interest rates. Changes in government debt as a percent of GDP explained 50 to 80 percent of the change in long-term real rates and 30 to 60 percent of the changes in short-term real rates.

---

[4] G-10 Deputies report, *op. cit.*

[5] Numerous empirical studies are available providing persuasive evidence of the increased integration of global capital markets. See J. Gagnon and M. Unferth, "Is There a World Real Interest Rate?" *Journal of International Money and Finance,* 1995; D. Pain and R. Thomas, "Real Interest Rate Linkages: Testing for Common Trends and Cycles," manuscript, Bank of England. 1995; and S. Cavaglia, "The Persistence of Real Interest Rate Differentials, A Kalman Filtering Approach," *Journal of Monetary Economics, 29* (June 1992).

Exhibit 10.2 Value of Independent Variables in World Real Interest Rates (G10 Less Switzerland).*

	Avg Real Interest Rates	Stock Prices	Oil Consumption		Narrow Money Growth		Govt Consumption	Govt Debt	Govt Deficit
		Stock T-1	dlt OILCY T-1	OILCY T-1	dlt M1 T-1	dlt M1 T-2	GCY T-1	RDEBTY T-1	RDEFY T-1
Medium Real Interest Rates (1959–73)	2.5	0.047	—	0.010	0.076	0.069	0.189	0.328	−0.003
Low Real Interest Rates (1974–79)	—	−0.107	0.002	0.026	0.089	0.092	0.167	0.278	—
High Real Interest Rates (1980–92)	3.9	0.093	−0.002	0.024	0.077	0.079	0.165	0.433	0.006

*GDP-weighted.

Average real interest rates: Government bond rates less centered moving average of CPI inflation. Stock: December-on-December changes in stock market prices less December-on-December CPI inflation. dlt Oilcy: Change in oil consumption as a proportion of GDP. Oilcy: Oil consumption as a proportion of GDP. dlt M1: Change in M1. Gcy: Current government consumption as a proportion of GDP. Rdebty: Real government debt as a proportion of GDP. Rdefy: Change in real debt (cyclically adjusted) as a proportion of GDP.

Data Source: J. Smith, (forthcoming), cited in Nigel Jenkinson "Savings, Investment and Real Interest Rates," *Bank of England Quarterly Bulletin* (February 1996).

An OECD study found that the rate of return on business capital was an important determinant of the level of real long-term interest rates. In fact, the study found that three-fourths of a percentage point of the total rise in real long-term interest rates, between the early eighties and 1994, was accounted for by the rise in the rate of return to capital in the G7 countries from 13 percent to 16 percent.[6]

It can be argued that the United States, as the major user of capital and a persistent demander of foreign capital, sets the level of real rates for the global economy. That is, U.S. Treasury debt instruments can be used as the benchmark for assessing the global real rate of return. It can also be argued that there is virtually no risk of default on U.S. Treasury debt instruments and, as such, they can be used as a proxy in constructing the real risk-free return to capital. Stripping out the inflation premium (see the next section) and the volatility premium, or the premium assessed to Treasuries due to the volatility of returns, enables the construction of a "real risk-free return to capital." Once the real risk-free return to capital has been determined, it can be used to construct appropriate real interest rates across markets.

SPREAD RELATIONSHIPS BETWEEN MARKETS

Country-specific real interest rates are influenced by the global real return to capital, domestic market return volatility and a "sovereign risk" premium. Assessment of the volatility premium is fairly straightforward, using historic total return volatility and the excess return demanded by the market per unit of volatility. Implied options volatility can also be used as a measure of local market volatility to derive a volatility premium.

The sovereign risk premium is more subjective and is related to the market's assessment of a specific-countries policy relative to the global market. In the study conducted by the three OECD economists, a country's past inflationary history, the level of public debt, the current

---

[6] Organization for Economic Cooperation and Development, "The Determinants of Real Long-Term Interest Rates: 17 Country Pooled-Time Series Evidence," by Adrian Orr, Malcolm Edey, and Michael Kennedy, OECD Working Paper No. 155, 1995.

Exhibit 10.3   Real Long-Term Interest Rate Determinants.

Variable	Coefficient
Return on Capital(1)	0.24
Portfolio Risk of Holding Bonds(2)	1.54
Inflation Blowout Risk Premium(3)	0.34
Current Account(4)	−0.15
Government Deficit(5)	0.15

Key: (1) Gross operating surplus of the enterprise sector divided by the capital stock. (2) Portfolio beta coefficient. A measure of the risk of holding bonds versus other securities. (3) Forward inflation minus trailing 10-year inflation. (4) Five-year trailing current account as a proportion of GDP. (5) Government deficit as a proportion of GDP.

Data Source: Organization for Economic Cooperation and Development, "The Determinants of Real Long-Term Interest Rates: 17 Country Pooled-Time-Series Evidence," by Adrian Orr, Malcolm Edey, and Michael Kennedy, OECD Working Paper, 1995.

account balance and the government deficit were identified as important factors in determining real long-term interest rate differentials among countries[7] (see Exhibit 10.3).

The OECD study clearly indicated that countries that have had an inflation credibility problem in the past continue to pay an inflation risk premium above what is implied by inflationary expectations. Increases in government debt as a percent of GDP will increase real long-term interest rates by 15 basis points for every 1 percent increase, and, if financed externally via the current account, is likely to be 30 basis points for every 1 percent increase. The empirical work of the OECD economists indicates that the inflation risk premium can be as high as one-third of a percentage point and remains in place for up to 10 years after forward inflation expectations have been adjusted.

The combined impact of high government debt–GDP and high current account–GDP can increase real rates by as much as 30 basis points according to the coefficients developed. Thus, for countries like Belgium and the Netherlands, which have high government debt–GDP levels but low current account–GDP ratios, the real rates are lower than for countries such as Australia, which experiences the reverse situation of

[7] *Ibid.*

Exhibit 10.4   "Real" 10-Year Government Bond Yields.

	U.S.	Japan	Germany	France	Italy	U.K.	Canada	G-10	Small OECD
1983	7.89	5.97	4.75	5.17	3.27	6.66	5.59	6.37	3.93
1984	8.14	5.00	5.57	5.64	4.95	6.31	8.38	6.71	4.41
1985	7.08	4.51	5.01	5.89	5.12	4.98	6.88	5.93	4.84
1986	5.78	4.61	6.31	6.20	5.31	6.62	4.95	5.52	5.57
1987	4.72	4.84	6.09	6.28	6.02	5.43	5.13	5.25	5.41
1988	4.77	4.04	5.23	6.34	6.25	4.89	5.81	5.01	5.08
1989	3.63	2.90	4.16	5.36	6.39	2.53	4.80	4.00	4.62
1990	3.18	3.90	6.04	6.73	7.47	2.26	5.99	4.42	4.75
1991	3.55	3.05	4.96	5.79	6.81	4.16	3.79	4.19	4.11
1992	4.00	3.48	3.81	6.26	8.00	5.32	6.54	4.65	5.76
1993	2.87	2.85	2.83	4.59	6.89	5.76	5.37	3.67	3.79
1994	4.52	3.57	4.25	5.61	6.57	5.66	8.30	4.83	5.58
1995	3.70	3.43	4.93	5.71	6.55	4.76	5.90	4.35	5.36
91–95 Avg	3.73	3.28	4.16	5.59	6.96	5.13	5.98	4.33	4.92
83–95 Avg	4.91	4.01	4.92	5.81	6.12	5.03	5.96	4.99	4.86

*Nominal yields minus 1-year forward inflation (CPI).
Data Source: Barclays de Zoete Wedd Securities Limited.

modest debt–GDP ratios but high current account–GDP levels. Canada suffers from the worst of both effects—high debt *and* current account ratios, and, consequently, relatively high real rates (see Exhibit 10.4).

INTEREST RATES AND THE INFLATION PREMIUM

Standard financial market theory argues that the inflation premium embedded in a long-duration financial instrument is based on a forward assessment of inflation prospects. Regression analysis of 10-year government bonds for the major markets over multiple time periods indicates, however, that financial markets' judgments regarding future inflation are heavily tempered by past experience. That is, there is persuasive empirical evidence that past inflation is more important in explaining the inflation premia in bonds than forward looking inflation estimates. From many perspectives, this is entirely rational. Often, inflation is reflective of central bank credibility and resolve, and, as such, past inflation is an important input into any assessment of future inflation. Take the recent case of France versus Germany. The French have been measurably more successful at controlling inflation in recent years than the Germans, but the inflation premium embedded in French bonds has remained persistently higher than in German bonds because of past experience and the credibility of the German Bundesbank.

Exhibit 10.5 sets out the econometric relationship between forward and trailing inflation and the inflation premium over various time periods for the G-5 countries.

The analysis indicates, with considerable uniformity, that past inflation explains approximately two-thirds of the inflation premium in 10-year government bonds, and forward inflation explains roughly one-third.

Exhibit 10.5   Econometric Assessment of Inflation Premia for G-5 10-Year Government Bonds.

	Extended Period*		January 1985–December 1993	
	Trailing Inflation Coefficient	Forward Inflation Coefficient	Trailing Inflation Coefficient	Forward Inflation Coefficient
France	.56	.44	.56	.44
Germany	.60	.40	.46	.54
Japan	.66	.34	.68	.32
United Kingdom	.71	.29	.69	.31
United States	.71	.29	.88	.12
Average	.66	.34	.65	.35

The CPI was used as the inflation measure. Twelve-month trailing inflation plus 12-month forward inflation figures were used in the regression exercise. (For some countries, longer time periods were suggested by regression analysis, but the longer time periods added little to the results and were dropped in favour of a uniform time period for all countries.) Realized 12-month forward inflation was used as a proxy for expected inflation. Coefficients generated were normalized to sum to 1.

*France, January 1985–February 1994; Germany, January 1975–February 1994; Japan, February 1985–February 1994; United Kingdom, June 1970–February 1994 and the United States, February 1974–January 1994.

YIELD CURVE SLOPE

As with the United States, the slope of the yield curve generally reflects the phase of the business cycle and the current stance of monetary policy. To the extent economies are in sync from a growth perspective, their respective yield curves should, all else being equal, be similarly shaped. Asynchronous growth between countries often creates differential investment opportunities where spreads between markets at different stages of the cycle can be exploited and where expected yield curve changes can be exploited in a global bond portfolio (see Exhibit 10.6).

Exhibit 10.6   Yield Curve Slope.

	U.S.	Japan	Germany	France	Italy	U.K.	Canada	G-10	Small OECD
1983	1.50	1.22	2.47	−0.39	0.46	1.11	1.93	1.25	1.06
1984	1.72	0.94	2.18	0.82	−0.07	1.26	1.55	1.47	0.61
1985	2.32	−0.13	1.82	0.67	−0.34	−1.19	1.29	1.11	0.31
1986	0.99	0.23	1.59	−0.78	−1.54	−0.86	0.03	0.35	0.27
1987	1.22	0.74	2.37	1.06	−0.40	−0.13	1.18	0.89	1.03
1988	0.86	0.30	2.14	1.04	0.31	−0.75	0.37	0.71	1.00
1989	−0.74	−0.28	−0.31	−0.67	0.80	−3.76	−2.19	−0.82	−0.67
1990	0.39	−0.82	0.24	−0.25	1.87	−3.06	−1.89	−0.17	−0.65
1991	1.98	−0.91	−0.82	−0.56	1.69	−1.38	0.86	0.54	−0.81
1992	3.25	0.86	−1.62	−1.86	−0.27	−0.44	1.59	1.22	−1.88
1993	2.57	1.20	−0.74	−1.64	1.16	1.48	2.37	1.34	−0.78
1994	2.34	1.96	1.61	1.52	2.20	2.53	2.94	2.17	1.78
1995	0.57	2.26	2.40	1.08	1.46	1.45	1.15	1.33	2.04
91–95 Avg	2.14	1.07	0.17	−1.46	1.25	0.73	1.78	1.32	0.07
83–95 Avg	1.46	0.58	1.03	0.00	0.56	−0.29	0.86	0.88	0.25

*Ten-year government bonds minus 3-month interest rates.
Data Source: Barclays de Zoete Wedd Securities Limited.

SELECTED REFERENCES

Cavaglia, S. "The Persistence of Real Interest Rate Differentials, A Kalman Filtering Approach." *Journal of Monetary Economics, 29* (June 1992).

Gagnon, J., and Unferth, M. "Is There a World Real Interest Rate?" *Journal of International Money and Finance,* 1995.

Group of Ten Deputies. "Savings, Investment and Real Interest Rates." October 1995.

Helbling, Thomas, and Wescott, Robert. "The Global Real Interest Rate," Staff Studies for the World Economic Outlook, International Monetary Fund.

Islam, Ifty. "Real Interest Rates," Global Fixed Income Research, Merrill Lynch, January, 1996.

Jenkinson, Nigel. "Saving, Investment and Real Interest Rates," *Bank of England Quarterly Bulletin* (February 1995).

Organization for Economic Cooperation and Development. "The Determinants of Real Long-Term Interest Rates: 17 Country Pooled-Time Series Evidence," by Adrian Orr, Malcolm Edey, and Michael Kennedy. OECD Working Paper No. 155, 1995.

Pain, D., and Thomas, R. "Real Interest Rate Linkages: Testing for Common Trends and Cycles." Manuscript, Bank of England. 1995.

Index